WORDS OF THANKS
TO **TIM KELLER**

At strategic moments, God sometimes makes a surprising choice of human instruments (Gideon, David, Saul of Tarsus). In our own time, I can't imagine a more appropriate choice of a leader than Tim Keller to represent our faith in the fishbowl that is New York City. By temperament, intellect, trustworthiness, and driving spirit, Tim is supremely qualified.
—PHILIP **YANCEY**

Thank you, Tim, for your willingness to coach a young banker into becoming a pastor and church planter. Your courage, godliness, tenacity, intellect, humility, and creativity have not only touched our lives but guided us as we modeled our church plant based on the best that we learned from the early days of Redeemer. Thousands have seen Jesus as a result, and that church has raised up a new generation of pastors and church plants. The ripple effect of your ministry in New York is uncountable. Tim and Kathy, thanks for sharing your encouragement and wisdom with us.
—ANDREW AND DONNA **FIELD**

Tim, thank you for modeling what it looks like for a minister's private integrity to match his public message. Thank you becoming more humble and open-handed, not less, with the ever-growing stature that the Lord has entrusted to you. Thank you for the friendship, guidance, vision, and availability when I have felt over my head. Thank you for welcoming the fruit of joy even—no, especially—in the awareness that our days are numbered.
—SCOTT **SAULS**

Tim, thank you for revealing the love and saving grace of Christ and for bringing us to faith. Your posture of humility, gift of teaching, and brilliance in connecting everyday life to Christ are unparalleled. You changed the trajectory of our lives, as you have for so many other people, giving us answers to questions we didn't even know how to ask, shepherding us in our search for truth, for meaning, for God. In that, you gave us the greatest gift, and we are deeply grateful.
—BILL AND GRETCHEN **KURTZ**

Tim, your preaching, writing, and church planting/building work in NYC has had an incredible impact on my wife and I for over two decades. I have been reading your books and continue to read the Proverbs and Psalms devotionals daily. In particular, your teaching on God's grace and *His* attitude towards the poor has been so important and practical. We are also so grateful for you and Kathy and the books you have collaborated on together. Your example has been very powerful to us in our marriage. Thank you for your faithfulness, your brilliance in communicating God's truth, and for the chance to collaborate on the Forums about Music and Faith. Much love to you, Kathy, and your family.
—JOHN **PATITUCCI**

Thank you, Tim, for the clear and steady voice you have been through the years. Thank you for the challenges and the encouragement. You have been a testament of what faithfulness to the end looks like. Thank you.
—C.J. **QUARTLBAUM**

Hey there Tim, did you know how often you speak to me? I have 252 of your Redeemer sermons on my laptop, and whenever I am seeking wisdom and encouragement, I pull up one of those. Your grace-filled message, in your voice, unfailingly lifts me up. I am truly blessed.
—FRANCIS **COLLINS**

Tim, thank you for living your life to glorify God. I was introduced to your books and ministry through the C.S. Lewis Institute, which started my journey into cultural apologetics. I am forever grateful for your gracious, brilliant defense of the Christian faith.
—ANNIE **NARDONE**

Tim, on behalf of all of us at the C.S. Lewis Institute in the US, Canada, and UK, I'd like to thank you for providing us and countless others with an approach to discipleship and apologetics which uses both reason and imagination, not unlike our namesake, C.S. Lewis. May your writings, sermons, and prophetic words like Lewis's continue to point people to Jesus Christ for decades to come!
—JOEL S. **WOODRUFF**

Tim, there are several times in my life where I was sick, pinned in a corner, self-absorbed, and utterly confused. I thank God your online sermons were a click away.
—CHARLIE **PEACOCK**

When we discovered your books and sermons, we had just sprung from an enthusiastic emergent church and landed in a Reformed church plant, where we were learning at last the language and history of our faith. Your words helped us see how Christianity fit with the world we saw around us and how we could carry our faith home with us on Sundays and live it out through our work, in our marriage, and, eventually, as parents. We have been profoundly blessed by your example and your faithfulness in ministry. Thank you for teaching us how the gospel touches every aspect of our lives and for showing us over and over again the beauty of our Redeemer.
—MITCH AND THÉA **ROSENBURG**

Your constant reminder that we are "more flawed than we imagine and yet more loved than we could ever hope," has humbled me around those I don't like or agree with, and assured me around those more savvy and smart than I.
—GLEN **KLEINKNECHT**

Thank you, Tim! Not only did you usher me into the freedom of the gospel, but you entrusted me with a vision to equip our church for gospel-centered work in a broken world. You were patient with my on-the-job theological and faith formation. And you made this pioneering ministry a church-wide priority. We've been blessed to see God use the crucible of work to draw hearts to him, as well as to transform people's sense of vocational calling. Thank you for leading us on this journey and working with me to paint a leaf.
—KATHERINE LEARY **ALSDORF**

Tim, your teaching and friendship have had a life-altering and enduring impact on me. Besides transforming how I understood the gospel and its implications on my life and business, your gentle, humble counsel and encouragement has lifted me during some critical crossroads of my life. Thank you for your faithful teaching and for the way you have modeled humble leadership of organizations and movements.
—MIKE **BONTRAGER**

Over the course of my life I've met people who have outstanding intellects and people who have compassionate pastoral hearts, but I have never met anyone who combines those two qualities quite like you do. You are a model to so many of us for so many reasons. You're a truth seeker, a peacemaker, and an institution builder. But you are also an extraordinary friend—kind and generous, authentic and vulnerable, always seeking to build others up. You've graced my life and my wife's in profound ways. We cherish you and Kathy and thank God in our every remembrance of you.
—PETER **WEHNER**

Thank you, Tim, for teaching me how to think and live in the heart of divine paradoxes, pointing to Jesus, and teaching me, "Yes!" I have been forever changed by your life and ministry.
—CHRIS **WHITFORD**

Tim: thanks for opening my eyes to a mercy and justice ministry.
For many years the churches I attended never taught me about God's heart for the poor and marginalized. Your teaching on this topic has ignited a life-long passion which created the original Hope for New York (and all the subsequent iterations in other cities, such as my current ministry, Hope for Miami). Further, you had the willingness to allow me to grow into this ministry vision and trusted me to lead it. I am forever grateful and the kingdom has expanded because of it.
—YVONNE DODD **SAWYER**

Our paths have crossed only obliquely, not in any way you would remember, but your influence has been significant. Through recordings, books, and occasional in-person events you have faithfully demonstrated how the Christian faith addresses the deepest issues of the human heart. That has been a huge encouragement at a time when so many powerful cultural crosscurrents buffet the church and people of faith. To use a phrase my mentor Francis Schaeffer was fond of, your example has been what I've needed to "keep on keeping on." Thank you for your faithfulness, your pastor's heart, your commitment to Holy Scripture, and for blessing me and so many others with your lovely and creative gifts over so many years.
—DENIS **HAACK**

Your ministry has affected me tremendously. When my husband and I helped plant a church, I led women's Bible studies using the studies you wrote for your church. I will forever cherish the discussions I had with women fostered by your materials. When I was soul-tired, I would listen to one of your sermons, which reminded me over and over again of God's heart of grace for me and kept me able to teach others. Thank you for being a dedicated student of God's Word and for sharing what you learned as you drew near to Him.

—JESSIE **KLASSEN**

Dear Tim, thanks for your friendship over the years. And thank you for your prophetic voice in an age of confusion. Barbara and I are praying for your recovery from cancer, a blessing in itself, but also a blessing to us all in that it would allow us to benefit from your wisdom for years to come.

—WILLIAM **EDGAR**

Months into the pandemic, I was confronted with a major decision. Isolated, I reached out and prefaced our phone conversation by saying, "Tim, you have been my pastor for so long, so I thought I would come to you to get some counsel." You immediately replied, "That's right, I am your pastor." You're known around the world for being a great preacher and teacher, but not too many people get to experience what a wonderful pastor you are. You modeled for me what it is like to have a shepherd who knows his flock and calls them by name. Over the years, I've consistently received wise counsel and profound teaching from you . . . thank you!

—JENNY C. **CHANG**

Tim, thank you for always making it clear that you serve as part of a team, not as an individual. Thank you for the model you gave us when you sought out pastors of different denominations to meet and pray together, and when you created a diaconate made up of deacons and deaconesses that could minister more fully to the women of Redeemer and to the city around us. Thank you for modeling the partnership of marriage, and for affirming the complement of Kathy's mind and faith by inviting her to join you in teaching and writing—it was always clear that Kathy was not only beside you but with you in ministry. Your example in this has impacted so many of us that were still single more than you will ever know.

—MARLENE HENSLEY **HUCKS**

Tim was my pastor from 1999 until he retired from the pulpit in 2017. I came to Redeemer in New York City at a particularly lean time in my life. His ministry—following Jesus' dictum to "feed my sheep"—deeply nourished my soul. He engaged my mind, softened my heart, and inspired my imagination. Tim was also God's instrument for much of the C.S. Lewis work I have been a part of over the past twenty years. My debt to him remains to this day.

—MAX **MCLEAN**

Thank you for planting Redeemer. It was the model for the church we helped to plant, and is now the home church for our children living in New York. And thank you for all of your books—but, of course, especially for your contribution to *It Was Good: Making Art to the Glory of God!*

—NED **BUSTARD**

Thank you for being a pastor to me, even though we have never met. I have listened to your sermon recordings one after another, diligently taking notes, rewinding, pausing to capture just how you phrased something. You have used your gift of words to communicate the truth with clarity and care, and for that I will be forever grateful.

—LAURIE **BERTRAND**

The song "There is a Redeemer" brings sweet memories of the formative decade I sat under your gospel-centered preaching. The freedom of the gospel increasingly guides my life as a scientist, filtering the world through a lens in which I see an intricate microscopic world that is beautiful ... yet broken and waiting to be restored. Thank you for preaching the gospel, and showing us how it applies to each day.

—JOHN **WU**

Tim and Kathy, your life and ministry have had an impact on mine in countless indirect ways, which, in being indirect, testify mightily to the power of your work and faithfulness over the years. Everywhere I go, I am blessed to work with, be edified by, and befriend those who have been shaped and formed by the Kellers. What greater legacy can there be than to influence those who go on to influence others, and so on, into eternity. I thank God for this kind of ministry. I thank God for you both.

—KAREN SWALLOW **PRIOR**

THE CITY FOR GOD

ESSAYS HONORING THE WORK OF
TIMOTHY KELLER

SQUARE HALO BOOKS

In Christian art, the square halo identified a living person presumed to be a saint. Square Halo Books is devoted to publishing works that present contextually sensitive biblical studies, and practical instruction consistent with the Doctrines of the Reformation. The goal of Square Halo Books is to provide materials useful for encouraging and equipping the saints.

©2021 Square Halo Books, Inc.
P.O. Box 18954
Baltimore, MD 21206
www.SquareHaloBooks.com

The cover photo of Tim Keller is by Nathan Troester. The cover photo of skyscrapers and the back page illustration are by Ned Bustard.

ISBN 978-1-941106-26-6
Library of Congress Control Number: 2022933936

Printed in the United States of America

CONTENTS

RUSSELL **MOORE**

Foreword

Thanks to Tim Keller, I felt really guilty.

Just a few minutes before, Tim Keller had interrupted his train of thought to say, "Hold on, Russell; Kathy's telling me something." I could barely hear her in the background but I could make out the words, "It's time to get off the phone; you've got to take your medicine." I could almost hear the smile in his words. "I'd better go; Kathy's making sure I follow doctor's orders," he said. "I'm going to get in trouble if I don't."

As I put down the phone I smiled at the sweetness of that—a wife making sure her husband is healthy; a husband playfully conversing with her; a couple obviously in love. But then I paused, as the guilt poured over me. I looked down at the phone and realized that we'd been talking for well over an hour. That part wasn't unusual. I was going through one of the most difficult times of my life, and Tim spent the entire time giving counsel and encouragement, as well as the welcome distraction of talking about Herman Bavinck's theology and Charles Taylor's philosophy and a new history of honor and shame in the first-century Roman Empire. That part wasn't unusual either. But I realized the date, and why he needed to take that medicine. He was going through another round of chemotherapy.

"You're an idiot!" I said to myself. "Why did you waste his time on your trivial problems, none of which amount to anything compared to fighting pancreatic cancer! Why didn't you just ask to pray with him?"

His treatments were really effective; the doctors were pleased. We have every reason to believe that we have years of Tim Keller yet with us. But, still: who spends time, during chemotherapy, thinking about checking on people who've never suffered in that way? Tim Keller does. And over the next few minutes I thought about the ways that Keller has done just that—for decades and decades. True, he didn't need to endure all those medicines and chemicals when he was setting out to plant Redeemer Presbyterian Church. That had to be an endurance contest all its own. Church planting is hard any-where—but church planting in New York City, with, of all things, an evangel-ical and Presbyterian church? Led by a pastor without the vibe of a celebrity or an entrepreneur? Tim Keller would have been well within his rights to say that his focus on that would keep him from worrying about others: about the next generation of church-planters, about the skeptics questioning the existence of God but who lived in Cairo or Kyoto or Cullman and who would never be known to him, about many of us who are writing sections of this book, and many who are reading it.

Tim Keller's ministry—past, present, and future—is important for global Christianity for a number of reasons. One reason is that God gave us his ministry, and equipped him to do it, at a crucial time in global Christianity. At a time of rapid secularization, the temptation for those of us who believe the gospel would be to try to wall off the outside world, to concentrate on narrower and narrower audiences of people most likely to give us a hearing.

Tim Keller, though, pioneered a way of church planting that was not ashamed of the gospel—and that wasn't threatened by those who would in-terrogate it with skepticism or even kick against it with hostility. He preached in such a way that the authority of Scripture was evident, and, with it, the way that Tim took his hearers seriously. He translated unfamiliar concepts for people who had never encountered them, and he did so without condescen-sion or without dumbing those concepts down. He easily could have accom-modated himself to evading the parts of the Christian message that would be most unpopular in an urban metropolitan setting. Or he could have ac-commodated himself to feeding the anger of the sort of Christians who want merely to denounce the people in those settings. Tim Keller always seemed to know that a non-Christian just might be a not-yet Christian—that the people around him were, like all of us, created, fallen, and in need of redemption and restoration. Through an ongoing lifetime of ministry, he reminds us that we have encountered a God who lives, a prodigal God who seeks us out and holds us fast. The tomb is really empty, the kingdom is really coming. There really is a City waiting for us whose foundations cannot be shaken. The sto-ries are true. The Good News is really good.

Ministry would have been easier for Tim Keller if he had done what many do. He could have put a "both/and" where Scripture puts an "either/or"— and downplayed the confrontation that comes when any person or culture is confronted by One who declares Himself to be the Way, the Truth, and the Life. Or he could have done what many others do. He could have put an "either/or" where the Bible puts a "both/and." But he instead offered up the "either/or" of the claims of Christ—helping people to know exactly who this God is that is revealed in the gospel of Jesus Christ. And he believed enough in the authority of Scripture, and the witness of the Christian church across the ages and places, to keep the "both/and" where God has placed it: both exposition and contextualization, both faith and fidelity, both evangelism and justice, both mind and heart, both conviction and compassion, both coming judgment and present mercy, both a longing for the kingdom of God and a desire for the flourishing of the cities around us. And—sometimes—both chemotherapy and ministry to those who need it.

Tim Keller will cringe if he reads this, and probably at many of the other essays too, expressing gratitude as they do. He's just a human being, he would tell us—and we know that. He's a sinner like everybody else—we know that. Anything that he's accomplished is all due to God's working, not his—and we know that too. But we also know that the God who tells us to pray for the welfare of the city has told us to give thanks to God for everything, and everyone, who, by His grace, points us back to Christ. And so, however much Tim Keller protests, we are willing to interrupt him. We don't feel guilty in saying:

Thanks to God, we have Tim Keller.

GOSPEL

SCOTT **SAULS**

Character

GENEROSITY AND GRACE

I first met Tim Keller in 2007. I believed it then—and I still believe—that he is the best English-speaking Christian preacher, thinker, and visionary of our time. I am not alone in this. But having also served alongside Tim and observed his leadership firsthand, I've found other things that I appreciate about him even more than those qualities. I suppose that now is a good time to remind myself and others about them, especially in light of his cancer diagnosis.

So here are a few important things that Tim's example taught me during my years at Redeemer (and also since that time):

First, in this weird and troubling age of Christian celebrity, where platform-building, fame-chasing, green-room-dwelling, and name-dropping can easily replace gospel virtues, Tim inspired me with his reluctance to participate in or even flirt with the trappings of Christian celebrity. He never chased the spotlight. He never tried to make a name for himself. The counsel of Jeremiah to his secretary—"Do you seek great things for yourself? Seek them not" (Jer. 45:5)—seemed like a life philosophy for Tim as well. Shy about himself and boastful about Jesus, his ambition was to advance Jesus' kingdom spiritually, socially, and culturally—whether through Redeemer or (notably) through promoting and supporting other churches and leaders.

Second, Tim waited until he was almost sixty years old to publish his first trade book. Humbly, he wanted to wait until he was old and wise enough to write the best possible book he could on any given subject. No doubt, his prolific writing since then has made up for lost time.

Third, in a time of posturing, comparing, and competing—a time when many pastors see each other as obstacles to overcome versus kingdom co-laborers to pray for and applaud—Tim has always been the latter. Instead of trying to position Redeemer as New York's Walmart of churches that would swallow up "the competition" with its superior offerings, Tim consistently leveraged time, resources, and energy to build a church planter training organization through which to bring more church planters, and with them more churches, into the city of New York. He was happy to see other NYC pastors succeed and other NYC churches thrive, even if it meant that Redeemer's "slice of the pie" might become smaller as a result. Tim never had a market share mentality about Christians in his city, and he never targeted members of other churches, either overtly or covertly, so as to lure them to his own church. Instead, he focused on reaching the unreached, paying special attention to the skeptic and the seeker. If someone left Redeemer for another church, Tim wouldn't get snippy or defensive about it but would say something like, "Well, that's a good thing. It's going to make _____ Church that much stronger. And that's what we want: for all the churches in New York to be stronger. Redeemer is a sending church, after all, and this includes sending some of our best members to other NYC area churches."

Fourth, even though Redeemer grew and grew (and grew and grew and grew) under his gifted leadership, Tim never embraced the mindset of "bigger and bigger." Rather, he emphasized quality of ministry over quantity of seats filled (ironically, under Tim's leadership it was virtually impossible to find a seat at the typical Redeemer service). Early on, his and Kathy's vision was to plant and pastor a small to medium-sized church in a single neighborhood of Manhattan, with maybe 350 or so people as their community. They didn't aspire for Redeemer to become a megachurch. Instead, they preferred to be one of many contributors to a broader movement of churches and denominations that would, together, serve their city. When Tim retired from Redeemer, he and Kathy talked about their hope that the future Redeemer would emerge into a movement that is not mega, but rather a network of numerous, well-contextualized, mid-size churches that serve New York's many unique neighborhoods. Tim finished pastoral ministry with the same mindset with which he started—not to turn Redeemer into a great church, per se, but rather to participate as contributors to a broader movement to make NYC a great city that resembles the city of God.

Fifth, as Tim's influence grew over the years, so did his dependence on and personal engagement with the hidden, ordinary graces such as daily Scripture reading and prayer. His long-time habit is to pray through Psalms every month and read the entire Bible every year. He also maintains, in his grandpa years, a youthful posture of learning that has him reading about 150 books per year. The prayer that I began praying for myself when I began writing books and serving as pastor of Christ Presbyterian—"Lord, give me character that is greater than my gifts, and humility that is greater than my influence"—was inspired chiefly by what I saw up close in Tim. Tim is the epitome of a phrase first coined by Nietzsche and later popularized by Eugene Peterson. His was and still is "a long obedience in the same direction."

Sixth, Tim and Kathy have a strong marriage. They live their lives together and not separate—face to face in friendship, and side by side in mission— and that makes such a difference. Rumor has it that they speak Tolkien's elvish language to each other in the privacy of their home (yes, they have some quirks). One of their favorite things to do is read and discuss books together. A little-known fact is that Kathy is equally as smart as Tim, if not smarter. As I understand it, Tim graduated second in his class at Gordon Conwell Theological Seminary. The person who graduated first was Kathy. No wonder their kids are all so intelligent.

Seventh, Tim is one of the best examples I have seen of meeting other people's flaws with the grace of the gospel. In five years of serving under his leadership, never once did I see him tear another person down to their face, on the Internet, or through gossip. Instead, he seemed to always assume the good in people. Occasionally, he would talk about how having the forgiveness and affirmation of Jesus frees us to "catch people doing good" instead of looking for things to criticize or be offended by. Even when someone had truly done wrong or been in error, Tim would respond with humble restraint and self-reflection instead of venting negativity and criticism. Tim was gracious toward people's flaws and sins—including mine on more than one occasion. He did this because that's what grace does. Grace reminds us that in Jesus we do not face the worst things about ourselves alone, but with a sympathetic companion who took God's wrath instead of us. Because Jesus has loved us like this, we of all people should restore reputations rather than destroy them, protect a good name instead of calling someone a name, shut down gossip instead of feeding gossip, and restore broken relationships rather than begrudging broken people.

Finally and perhaps most significantly, Tim could receive criticism, most of which came from the outside and was almost always unfair. But criticism would bring out the best in him rather than bringing out the worst in him. By his words and example, he taught me that getting defensive about criticism rarely, if ever, leads to healthy outcomes. He also taught me that our critics, including the ones who mischaracterize and falsely accuse us as pastors, can sometimes be God's instruments to teach and humble us as persons.

Perhaps an anecdote will help drive home the point here. In Tim's own words:

> If the criticism comes from someone who doesn't know you at all (and often this is the case on the internet) it is possible that the criticism is completely unwarranted and profoundly mistaken. I am often pilloried not only for views I do have, but also even more often for views (and motives) that I do not hold at all. When that happens, it is even easier to fall into a smugness and perhaps be tempted to laugh at how mistaken your critics are. "Pathetic…" you may be tempted to say. Don't do it. Even if there is not the slightest kernel of truth in what the critic says, you should not mock them in your thoughts. First, remind yourself of examples of your own mistakes, foolishness, and cluelessness in the past, times in which you really got something wrong. Second, pray for the critic, that he or she grows in grace.[1]

Several years after writing these words, Tim was awarded the esteemed Kuyper Prize at the Abraham Kuyper Center for Public Theology at Princeton Theological Seminary—until he was not. The prize, given to a single recipient annually since 1998, was designated to Tim for the excellence with which he has consistently modeled application of Kuyper's theology that declares God's ownership of "every square inch" (as Kuyper himself put it) of the created universe. Whether in business, the arts, politics, journalism, or other areas of influence, Tim has encouraged and empowered men and women to integrate their faith and their work, such that the lordship of Christ is brought to bear not only in private religious spaces, but also in public spheres of influence and the marketplace of ideas. Tim's application of Kuyper in his teaching and ministry has been so pervasive over the years that he was named in 2018 to *Fortune* magazine's "World's 50 Greatest Leaders" list.[2]

Although Tim was more than qualified for the Kuyper Prize, a backlash arose from several students and faculty in the Princeton community after he was announced as the esteemed recipient. The backlash was related to Tim's views on sex, marriage, and women's ordination, which sit on the historic-traditional side of the theological continuum. As a result of the complaints the seminary received, the award was rescinded, based on criteria that would have also eliminated Abraham Kuyper himself from consideration, and instead given to a recipient who represented Princeton's majority views on these matters. Nevertheless, the Kuyper Center asked Tim to lecture at the conference where the award was given to someone else. Tim graciously agreed.[3]

In an op-ed following Princeton's announcement to retract the award given to Tim, Katherine Alsdorf, cofounder of New York City's Center for Faith & Work, reflected on the announcement:

> [Tim and I] partnered in the establishment of the Center for Faith & Work, which may have done as much as any church in decades to honor Abraham Kuyper's vision of humble, respectful engagement in a world of many faith perspectives. His teaching combines a deep confidence that the gospel can change everything from our hearts, making us more humble and generous, to the institutions and society around us. While he would never have sought a "Kuyper award," I can't imagine anyone more worthy of it.
>
> Like some of the women who have objected and instigated the withdrawal of this award by Princeton Theological Seminary, I do not share Tim's complementarian views. However, I am deeply saddened by the tone of these objections, more so by the final effect.[4]

Depending on our particular perspective, we will all be moved in different ways by stories like this one. As for me, I am both touched and inspired by Tim's remarkable graciousness, as well as Katherine's humble, mature willingness to accept leadership from Tim for a higher good, even though they are not in full agreement even on things that are deeply important to them both. Each of them, in his or her own way, demonstrates for us what a gentle answer that comes from Christ can look like.

When I moved my family to New York City in 2007, I thought I was going to get to serve alongside and learn from one of the greatest preachers and visionary leaders of our time. And I did get to do that, along with a few others. But even more than this, the man gave me (and us) what M'Cheyne said is the most important thing a minister can give to his people—his own holiness. For me, Tim's life has painted notable pictures of integrity that exceeds imperfections, character that exceeds giftedness, prayerfulness that exceeds pragmatism, other-centeredness that exceeds personal ambition, generosity that exceeds personal comfort, and humility that exceeds (even a stellar) impact.

And now, Tim is beginning to paint for us a picture of what it can look like to finish well. He is providing glimpses of what it can look like to say with one's life and not merely with one's lips, "I am, and always have been, unworthy to untie the straps on Jesus' sandals. He must increase, and I must become less."

And yet, in becoming less, the man is becoming more. For as the man himself has said in sermons, "The less we presume to act like kings, the more like kings we shall be."

Thank you, Tim, for helping me want to be a better pastor, communicator, and leader. More than this, thank you for helping me want to be a better man. I know that you're not done running the race, and that there is more to come from you as you continue your faithful work, in whatever form that may take. As for me, I am grateful for how God has taught me these and other valuable things through you. And so I thank you, sir.

ENDNOTES

1   Timothy Keller, "How Do You Take Criticism of Your Views?", *Timothy Keller* (website), December 16, 2009, https://timothykeller.com/blog/2009/12/16/how-do-you-take-criticism-of-your-views.

2   "The World's 50 Greatest Leaders," *Fortune,* April 19, 2018, https://fortune.com/worlds-greatest-leaders/2018/.

3   Celeste Kennel-Shank, "Princeton Seminary cancels award to Tim Keller, but not his lecture," *The Christian Century,* April 4, 2017, https://www.christiancentury.org/article/princeton-seminary-cancels-award-tim-keller-not-his-lecture.

4   Katherine Leary Alsdorf, "OpEd: Tim Keller hired women in leadership," *A Journey Through NYC Religions,* March 29, 2017, https://nycreligion.info/oped-tim-keller-put-charge-train-men-women-leadership/.

SEAN MICHAEL **LUCAS**

Rhetoric

PREACHING TO THE HEART

"Unless the truth is not only clear but also *real* to listeners, then people will still fail to obey it," Tim Keller observed in his book on preaching. "Preaching cannot simply be accurate and sound. It must capture the listeners' interest and imaginations; it must be compelling and penetrate to their hearts."[1] While Keller has modeled this in his ministry, it is striking how often contemporary Presbyterian and Reformed preaching contents itself with *simply* being accurate and sound. The impression that the regular churchgoer receives from such sermons is that the most important factors in the Christian life are theological precision and exegetical correctness. Unwittingly, such Presbyterian men and women pursue theological accuracy as an end in itself, but the sad result is knowledge that "merely flits in the brain," rather than taking deep "root in the heart."[2]

The best theologians in the Reformed tradition knew differently. If truth was to transform, the mind certainly needed to apprehend certain facts, but the heart needed to be persuaded.[3] While the sixteenth-century Reformer John Calvin taught this, perhaps the best Reformed teacher of how truth must penetrate to the heart was the eighteenth-century pastor Jonathan Edwards. Throughout his twenty-three-year ministry in Northampton, Massachusetts, Edwards modeled an approach to Christianity generally and to preaching especially that recognized that truth must penetrate the human heart to bring genuine transformation. In fact, Edwards utilized a rhetorical strategy that relied on sensations formed during the preaching moment, which in turn raised affections and engaged the will to produce new virtuous practices. This "rhetoric of sensation" was essential as Edwards sought to capture his listeners' interests and imaginations and to advance biblical Christianity in his own time. Perhaps by paying attention to this old Reformed master, we might see a similar advance in our own time.[4]

THE PRESUPPOSITION: WHAT TRUE RELIGION IS

Right at the heart of the Great Awakening was the question of the nature of true religion.[5] While some believed that the true religion was best evidenced by doctrinal fidelity and others by moral rectitude, Edwards came up with a different answer. In *Religious Affections*, he famously argued that "true religion, in great part, consists in holy affections." In order to understand what Edwards meant, we first have to understand what he meant by affections. Affections are not really emotions or feelings; rather, "the affections are no other than the more vigorous and sensible exercises of the inclination and will of the soul."[6]

What does that mean? The answer is rooted in Edwards's ontology, or philosophy of being. For Edwards, in order for something to have *being* or existence, understanding and will were required. And being—summed up in the interplay between understanding and will—founded its expression in habit or disposition. As philosophical theologian Sang Hyun Lee explained, habits are not thoughtless ways in which actions are carried out; rather, "the habit of mind, for Edwards, functions as the very possibility of rationality and moral action . . . Habit is, rather, an active tendency that governs and brings about certain types of events and actions."[7]

It is important to recognize that Edwards used other words to stand in for habit, or disposition, including *inclination, temper, principle of nature,* and *sense of the heart.* So, when he defined the affections as "the more vigorous and sensible exercises of the inclination and will of the soul," it was the same thing as saying that *the affections are the exercises of habit or disposition that have been moved to act by sensation.* Sensations stir affections, which in turn stimulate the exercise of habit. Of course, not all affections are necessarily positive—hatred, for example, is an affection, but not frequently a "positive" one. Likewise, not all affections are vigorous—one might have affections that prove fleeting. Yet if one wants to understand what affections are, one would do well to see affections and actions connected together—and sensations are what move the affections to action.

Yet Edwards actually said that "true religion, in great part, consists in *holy* affections." What are *holy* affections? When a spiritual or religious sensation brings about the exercise of one's will (or habit, disposition, or inclination— Edwards used all these words as synonyms) so that the individual obeys God, that is a holy affection. And holy affections are found in the heart, which is the individual's center of thinking, feeling, and doing: "That religion which God requires, and will accept," Edwards wrote, "does not consist in weak, dull, and lifeless wouldings, raising us but a little above a state of indifference:

God, in his Word, greatly insists upon it, that we be in good earnest, fervent in spirit, and our hearts vigorously engaged in religion." Some of these holy affections include godly fear, hope in God and in his word, love to God and the people of God, holy hatred for sin, holy desire for God and holiness, holy joy, religious sorrow and mourning, gratitude and praise to God, compassion and mercy, and holy zeal. However, of all these affections, the greatest is love. Edwards called love "the chief of the affections and fountain of all other affections." In fact, "the essence of all true religion lies in holy love," and love sums "the whole of religion."[8]

As our hearts are affected with holy love or some other affection, the will moves to engage in holy practices—this is true religion. "Gracious and holy affections have their exercise and fruit in Christian practice," Edwards held. "They have that influence upon him who is the subject of 'em that they cause that a practice, which is universally conformed to, and directed by Christian rules, should be the practice and business of his life." True religion consists in holy affections, but these holy affections are "effectual in practice." Affections and practice *must* go together: "The power of godliness is exerted in the first place within the soul, in the sensible, lively exercise of gracious affections there. Yet the principal evidence of this power of godliness, is in those exercises of holy affections that are practical, and in their being practical." Affections that do not produce holiness in practical ways in daily living are not holy affections and do not represent true religion.[9]

THE MEANS: PREACHING

If, then, holy affections and resultant holy practices are at the heart of true religion, how do these holy affections get raised? Edwards believed that preaching was God's appointed means for stirring holy affections and moving people to faith and obedience. As he declared in a sermon preached at an ordination of a new pastor, "The preaching of the gospel by faithful ministers is the principal means that God makes use of for the exhibiting [of] Christ and his love and benefits to his elect people, and the chief means of their being sanctified, and so fitted to enjoy their spiritual bridegroom." As pastors preach the pure Gospel, their preaching would serve "as the great means of bringing about the prosperity and joy of the church." And so, preaching stirs love and joy, affections that move the will to follow Christ. Yet it is only through the preaching of "the pure unadulterated word of God" that pastors rightly raise the affections. As they preach God's word, they serve as pure conduits of God's grace to the human heart, stirring to new ways of living.[10]

Those who preach the word display both divine light and holy heat for the benefit of their hearers' souls. In one ordination sermon, Edwards noted that the excellency of a gospel minister was his ability to bring divine light to the minds of his congregants. The pastor's teaching and preaching must be clear and pure, evidencing a mastery of the Scriptures. But preaching also needed to demonstrate a "fervent zeal" that could be seen "in the earnestness, and power with which he preaches the word of God, declares to sinners their misery, and warns them to fly from the wrath to come, and reproves, and testifies against all ungodliness." If a pastor simply entertained "his auditory with learned discourses, without a savor of the power of godliness, or any appearance of fervency of spirit, and zeal for God and the good of souls, he may gratify itching ears, and fill the heads of his people with empty notions; but will not be very likely to reach their hearts, or save their souls." Divine light and holy heat—both are necessary for preaching to be effective.[11]

Of course, in preaching this way, pastors were simply imitating Jesus' own preaching. Edwards urged pastors to "imitate him in the manner of his preaching; who taught not as the scribes, but with authority, boldly, zealously and fervently; insisting chiefly on the most important things in religion ... insisting not only on the outward, but also the inward and spiritual duties." And so, not only was Jesus the substance of preaching, but the example of what preaching should be: for Jesus too preached to the heart. In the end, too, His own shed blood for humans' salvation offered a continuing inducement to preach in order to raise affections and "to impress their minds" with Christ.[12]

Edwards repeatedly defended this understanding of preaching during his ministry—preaching served to raise the affections through impressing the heart in the preaching moment. For example, in *Some Thoughts*, he claimed that "the main benefit that is obtained by preaching is by impression made upon the mind in the time of it, and not by an effect that arises afterwards by a remembrance of what was delivered." That is not to say that later remembrance was unimportant—but even the later remembrance was one of remembering the impression that was made. In other words, it is not the content recalled that is vital about the preaching moment, but the impression made, the affections raised, and the actions changed.[13]

Edwards defended styles of preaching that were passionate and that sought to make an impression. While some might object to "a great appearance of earnestness in voice and gesture," such objections were not well-made. To be sure, holy affections are raised properly through an appeal to truth. Yet "an exceeding affectionate way of preaching about the great things of religion has

... a much greater tendency to beget true apprehensions of them," especially when compared to "a moderate, dull, indifferent way of speak of 'em." And this was because a more affectionate way of preaching concerning the great truths of Scripture demonstrated a congruence with the glory and wonder of those truths: as "the true representation" of such matters, a passionate style "has most of a tendency to beget true ideas of it in the minds of those to whom the representation is made." Indeed, Edwards believed it was his duty "to raise the affections of my hearers as high as possibly I can, provided that they are affected with nothing but truth, and with affections that are not disagreeable to the nature of what they are affected with."[14]

THE STRATEGY: A RHETORIC OF SENSATION

Because preaching was God's ordained means for raising the affections and directing them to Christ, the preacher needed to understand how this was done. Edwards firmly believed that rhetoric could be used to create sensations—sensible knowing—which would stir the affections and move the will to action. Historian Perry Miller noted this long ago when he argued that Edwards knew that "the word must be pressed, and rhetoric must strive for impression; it is a strength, not a weakness of language, that no matter how sensational it becomes, it has to depend upon something happening to the recipient outside and above its own mechanical impact." As the preacher in the sermon presses upon the conscience with carefully chosen rhetoric, he strives for impression. Ultimately, the affections that arise—love or hate, joy or sorrow—must lead to holy actions, but it is the impression in the preaching moment that matters.[15]

Such a commitment to a rhetoric of sensation and affectionate preaching is why we should doubt claims that Edwards was a flat, monotone, or otherwise disengaged preacher. As historian George Marsden suggested, while Edwards did not have the dramatic gestures of George Whitefield or the intensity of Gilbert Tennent, and while he may have preferred to look at the back of the sanctuary rather than in the eyes of his parishioners, "through sheer intensity he generated emotion." The intensity was certainly driven by his own personality, but also through his rhetorical strategy. He desired for his words to carry weight, to create sensations, to raise affections, to move to action.[16]

Such intensity and emotion can be recognized in two sermonic examples, each of which created sensations that would raise the affections, which in turn would move the will. Most famously, Edwards's sermon "Sinners in the Hands of an Angry God" invoked sensations of judgment that sought to raise the affection of fear and cause the hearer to put her trust in Christ.

In "Sinners," Edwards sought to awaken hearers not simply to the *specula-tive* knowledge of hell—that is, an intellectual knowing that God will judge sinners, that He will do so in a place called hell, that this judgment will be torment that will last forever. Rather, Edwards desired to awaken sinners to a *sensible* knowledge of hell as well as the impeding reality that they could go there. Further, Edwards also desired for "Sinners" to awaken in his hearers a sense of their utter helpless to save themselves: if they were to be rescued from hell, their rescue must come from outside of themselves.

For example, Edwards warned that judgment was impending and would come at an unexpected time. "The unseen, unthought of ways and means of persons going suddenly out of the world are innumerable and inconceiv-able," he declared. Some sinners walk over hell unaware that the covering is rotten and so weak that it could collapse at any moment and send them straight to hell; others are in danger of arrows of death (no small problem in a territory surrounded by hostile Native Americans) that might strike them and send them to God's judgment. A collapsing cover or a deadly arrow—who knows when judgment might come?[17]

Certainly, God knows when such judgment might come because "natural men are held in the hand of God over the pit of hell; they have deserved the fiery pit, and are already sentenced to it, and God is dreadfully provoked." In fact, God's wrath is like "black clouds of God's wrath now hanging directly over your heads, full of the dreadful storm, and big with thunder"; it is like "great waters that are dammed for the present"; it is like a great bow of wrath that is bent and aimed at the sinner. For every sinner, God holds them "over the pit of hell, much as one holds a spider, or some loathsome insect, over the fire, abhors you, and is dreadfully provoked." Sinners might not recognize this is their condition—"you probably are not *sensible* of this"—but this is the reality. [18]

This piling on of images—fiery pit, thunder clouds, water dam about to break, wrathful bow, dangling spider—was meant awaken sensible knowl-edge that would raise the affection of fear and that would drive the individual to Christ. These sensations of judgment were one tool that Edwards used, but another strategy was to use sensations of delight to woo and win people to Christ. Perhaps the clearest example of this strategy was Edwards's ser-mon, "Heaven is a World of Love." As in the judgment sermon, in "Heaven" Edwards wants not simply to give speculative knowledge of heaven, but sen-sible knowledge: he wants his hearers' affections to be raised as they long for, desire, thirst, and hunger for heaven. Through these sensations of delight,

Edwards comforts his people but also creates hope, a profound expectation that these things are so for believers in Christ. This delight, comfort, and hope would produce holy obedience and faithful action.

In heaven, Edwards declared, believers will know God's glory as it "is manifested and shines forth in full glory, in beams of love; there the fountain overflows in streams and rivers of love and delight, enough for all to drink at, and to swim in, yea, so as to overflow the world as it were with a deluge of love." Not only will believers swim in the glory and love of God, but they will know perfect harmony with one another—as in a great orchestra, "there shall be no string out of tune to cause any jar in the harmony of that world, no unpleasant note to cause any discord." Holy love and harmony are among the chief delights of heaven, described as an ocean, a fountain, a sunbeam, an orchestra.[19]

Heaven too is like "a garden of pleasures, a heavenly paradise fitted in all respects for an abode of heavenly lovers, a place where they may have sweet society and perfect enjoyment of each other's love." Not only will heaven be a garden of pleasures, but "holy pleasure shall be as a river which ever runs, and is always clear and full." This river of delight comes in a world where it is always springtime, where every plant "shall be in perpetual bloom with the same undecaying pleasantness and fragrancy, always spring forth, always blossoming, and always bearing fruit." This is a garden of love, a world of delight, a place where God's love reigns in and through His people. Surely, this is a place where God's people long to be, a place for which the soul desires. Again, the piling up of images creates delightful sensations that raise holy affections that should produce holy practices and genuine transformation.[20]

Both through sensations of judgment and delight, Edwards utilized this rhetorical strategy of sensation in order to raise the affections and to move people to action. For those under the fearful expectation of judgment, the sermon's applications urged them to place their trust in Jesus Christ. For those whose heart has been raised to delight or longing, the sermon's applications urged sinners to faith in Christ and saints to live lives of love in anticipation of being in heaven, the world of love.

THE GOAL: HOLY AFFECTIONS AND PRACTICE

In the end, the goal of Edwards's preaching to the heart was the increase of holy affections, which would in turn lead to holy practice. And that was because preaching to the heart produced sensations that would in turn lead to exercises of the inclination and will of the soul. Not to preach to the heart, not to produce sensations that would lead to vigorous exercises of the will was to fail to preach properly. Quite simply, it was a waste of time. For the goal of the gospel minister is genuine piety, which is found in the center of one's being, the heart: "True piety is nothing remaining only in the head, or consisting in any speculative knowledge or opinions, or outward morality or forms of religion; it reaches the heart, is chiefly seated there, and burns there."[21]

While Edwards believed in preaching to the heart and utilized his strategy of sensation to do so, he recognized that in the end, the Holy Spirit was the only one who could truly raise the affections of God's people. "This inward burning of the heart that we speak of," Edwards declared, "is the exercise of grace in the heart and therefore must be that which is of a holy nature; 'tis the breathing and acting of the Spirit of God in the heart and therefore it must needs be holy and pure." The Spirit does His work in the hearts of the people, but also in the heart of the preacher: the Spirit warms the heart and fills it "with a great sense of those things that are to be spoken of, and with holy affections, that that sense and those affections may suggest words." The preacher preaches out of the holy affections that the Spirit has raised in order to raise the holy affections of God's people.[22]

In those times when proclamation becomes the word of God, when the Spirit takes the word and applies it immediately to the soul, when holy affections lead to holy practice—this is what every preacher longs for: "God's people sometimes set under the preaching of the Word with ardent and enflamed hearts; there is sometimes a sweet inward ardency of mind under the hearing of the Word." In those times, "the soul seems as it were to drink in the words of the minister as they come from his mouth, one sentence after another touches their hearts and things are alive, the heart is kindled, there is an inward warmth, the heart is fixed and the affections are active." In these holy moments, as affections are raised and the will exercised, the Spirit brings about genuine transformation through the ministry of the word.[23]

The great desire that Presbyterian and Reformed pastors—along with those from the broader evangelical tradition—ought to have is for their preaching to penetrate to their hearers' hearts. As the great theologians of the Reformed tradition suggest, only in this way will preaching accomplish its purpose. Thus we find that the point that Tim Keller made at the beginning of this essay—that truth must become real to the hearer through the engagement of the heart—is exactly the same as his mentor Jonathan Edwards: "Our people don't so much need to have their heads stored, as to have their hearts touched; and they stand in need of that sort of preaching that has the greatest tendency to do this."[24]

ENDNOTES

1   Timothy Keller, *Preaching: Communicating Faith in an Age of Skepticism* (New York: Dutton, 2015),
    157 (emphasis his). It is a great honor to contribute to this book honoring Tim's ministry. My first con-
    nection with him (which I doubt he'd remember) came when I managed the Westminster Seminary
    Bookstore back in the late 1990s; I was one of his suppliers of volumes from the *Works of Jonathan Ed-
    wards*! He also gave one of the keynote addresses at a 1998 Jonathan Edwards conference in Lancaster,
    PA, that my friend Steve Nichols and I organized. It seemed fitting to come back to our mutual mentor,
    Jonathan Edwards, in order to honor him and his ministry.

2   John Calvin, *The Institutes of the Christian Religion*, ed. J.T. McNeill (Philadelphia: Westminster, 1960),
    1.5.9, 61–62.

3   Calvin, *Institutes*, 1.2.1, 40..

4   This essay draws from the insight first offered in Perry Miller, "The Rhetoric of Sensation," in *Errand
    into the Wilderness* (Cambridge: Harvard University Press, 1956), 167–183.

5   See Sean Michael Lucas, "'What is the Nature of True Religion?': *Religious Affections* and Its American
    Puritan Context," in *All for Jesus: A Celebration of the 50th Anniversary of Covenant Theological Semi-
    nary*, ed. Robert A. Peterson and Sean Michael Lucas (Ross-faire, UK: Christian Focus, 2006), 117–136.

6   Jonathan Edwards, *The Works of Jonathan Edwards, vol. 2: Religious Affections*, ed. John E. Smith (New
    Haven: Yale University Press, 1959), 95, 96.

7   This paragraph and the next reproduces material in a slightly altered form from Sean Michael Lucas,
    God's Grand Design: The Theological Vision of Jonathan Edwards (Wheaton, IL: Crossway, 2011), 92–93.
    The Lee quotes are from Sang Hyun Lee, *The Philosophical Theology of Jonathan Edwards* (Princeton, NJ:
    Princeton University Press, 1988), 8, 35.

8   This paragraph reproduces material in slightly altered form from Lucas, *God's Grand Design*, 94. The
    Edwards material comes from Edwards, *Religious Affections*, Yale, 2:99, 102–107, 118–119..

9   Edwards, *Religious Affections*, 383, 393.

10 Jonathan Edwards, "The Church's Marriage to her Sons, and to Her God," in *The Works of Jonathan Ed-
    wards, vol. 25: Sermons and Discourses, 1743-1758*, ed. Wilson H, Kimnach (New Haven: Yale University
    Press, 2006), 185, 171; Edwards, "Sons of Oil, Heavenly Lights," in Yale, 269–270.

11 Edwards, "True Excellency of a Minister of the Gospel," Yale, 25:92, 96.

12 Edwards, "Christ the Great Example of Gospel Ministers," Yale, 25:339; Edwards, "Christ's Sacrifice an
    Inducement to His Ministers," Yale, 25:672.

13 Jonathan Edwards, "Some Thoughts on the Revival of Religion," in *The Works of Jonathan Edwards, vol.
    4: The Great Awakening*, ed. C.C. Goen (New Haven: Yale University Press, 1972), 397.

14 Edwards, "Some Thoughts," *The Great Awakening*, 386–387.

15 Perry Miller, "The Rhetoric of Sensation," 183.

16 George M. Marsden, *Jonathan Edwards: A Life* (New Haven: Yale University Press, 2003), 220.

17 Jonathan Edwards, "Sinners in the Hands of an Angry God," in *The Works of Jonathan Edwards, vol. 22:
    Sermons and Discourses, 1739-1742*, ed. Harry S. Stout and Nathan O. Hatch, with Kyle P. Farley (New
    Haven: Yale University Press, 2003), 407.

18 Edwards, "Sinners," Yale, 22: 409, 410, 411 (emphasis mine).

19 Jonathan Edwards, "Heaven is a World of Love," in *The Works of Jonathan Edwards, vol. 8: Ethical Writ-
    ings*, ed. Paul Ramsey (New Haven: Yale University Press, 1989), 370, 371.

20 Edwards, "Heaven," Yale, 8: 382, 383.

21 Edwards, "True Excellency of a Minister of the Gospel," Yale, 25:89.

22 Jonathan Edwards, "Sermon on Luke 24:32," in *Works of Jonathan Edwards Online, vol. 51: Sermons,
    Series II, 1736* (Jonathan Edwards Center at Yale University, 2008); Jonathan Edwards, "Sermon on
    Matt. 13:3–4(a)," in *Works of Jonathan Edwards, Online, vol. 56: Sermons, Series II, July–December 1740*
    (Jonathan Edwards Center at Yale University, 2008); Edwards, "Some Thoughts," Yale, 4:437.

23 Edwards, "Sermon on Luke 24:32".

24 Edwards, "Some Thoughts," 388.

ANNIE **NARDONE**

Apologetics

LEWIS, KELLER, AND THE GOSPEL

[C.S. Lewis] possessed to an astonishing degree the gift of saying what needed to be said clearly and briefly."
—Walter Hooper, introduction to *Present Concerns*[1]

Brevity *is* the soul of wit,[2] and applied to apologetics, brevity in words that reach the soul conveys the essence of theological answers. C.S. Lewis's influence on Tim Keller's ministry is evident: both use a similar apologetics style of clarity, tackling the heart of skepticism and imaginatively answering the "mere" questions about the Christian faith. The ongoing popularity of their writing vitally speaks to the hearts of believers and nonbelievers. Those in the field of cultural apologetics look to their creative example to connect with today's religiously divided culture.

Mainline churches are fractionalized over different doctrine, placing themselves in danger of taking a human-centered rather than God-centered theological approach. Lewis aptly notes that "One of the things Christians are disagreed about is the importance of their disagreements."[3] Disagreements over dogma are not a critical first step when we share our faith; the important thing to focus on is the underlying doubt. So often we are hasty to throw a Scripture passage at someone who has no context or knowledge of biblical matters. Our human-centered response is often expediency rather than a truly engaging conversation.

There was not a time in my life in which God was absent. My parents and I attended the Presbyterian church in my hometown, and "big church" (what I called the regular service with my parents) followed Sunday School. Children's choir, confirmation, and Summer Bible School played a part in my young life. As an adult, my faith was a perception that God was real and near. Calvin called this the *sensus divinitatis*—a sense of divinity. At times, that sense of holiness was pushed away or buried; still, His existence was always undeniably present. But that innate (and sometimes nagging) sense also fostered questions that seemed to contradict what I had been taught as a child. Is the text of the Bible literally true, every last bit? Why would God allow me to be hurt? Perhaps the innate sense that there is a God is what draws the skeptic and believer to the church.

In Lewis and Keller, I discovered Christian thinkers to whom I could relate. To many Christians it seems that genuine faith carries with it certain frustrating expectations—like a workbook awaiting neatly pat answers—or an expected persona that we know we cannot attain. We doubt, and then feel ashamed of our doubt. Lewis and Keller give well-reasoned responses that are clear and sensible, not cluttered with trite answers followed by a verse taken out of context. They are the apologists for the common man who has questions; they challenge the skeptics to think through their own doubts and arguments as well.

During World War II (1942–1944), C.S. Lewis presented a series of BBC radio shows in England that aired with a "popular or familiar tone,"[4] delivering his message not as a man of letters, but as a layman who related to his ordinary audience. George Marsden, Professor of History at University of Notre Dame, states, "When it came to speaking on the BBC to just about every sort of person, he knew where to begin—with our common sense that there is a right and a wrong. And unlike what one might expect of a university don, he could speak in simple terms that just about everyone could understand."[5]

These talks were published in 1952 as *Mere Christianity*. It is not difficult to imagine that living through the chaos of bombings, air raids, and unrepentant evil would prompt people to ask basic questions about God. The broadcasts and book resonated with people from different paths—academics and chimney sweeps, young people and their grandparents, those who stood firm in their faith and others who had big questions. The all-encompassing beauty of Lewis's explanations are still meaningful because they are illustrative—coaxing understanding through imagination, communicated in a poetic and plain-spoken way, similar to storytelling and the parables Christ shared in the New Testament.

Decades after *Mere Christianity* was published, Tim Keller wrote *The Reason for God* in response to the culture's modern-day skepticism and included "a more positive exposition of the faith,"[6] revealing that our fears and questions about truth, suffering, morality, and scientific arguments remain consistent through time. When asked if Lewis was a one-time or ongoing

influence in his own life and ministry, Keller confirms, "Ongoing, for two reasons ... he saw where western civilization was going. In *The Abolition of Man*,
he was remarkable in anticipating postmodernism ... He was a man of the
imagination. He didn't tackle dated issues. He had knowledge of intellectual
trends with the ability to speak pictorially. And he [Lewis] helps me to go not
necessarily to the particular issue, but to look at the underlying mindset."[7]
That "underlying mindset" is what the church often fails to examine.

A mark of a brilliant theological mind is the ability to convey a difficult
idea like the problem of evil so clearly and matter-of-factly that anyone can
understand. Skeptics do not come to church to inquire about young earth versus old earth philosophy or the day of creation. They ask why there's an earth
at all. Lewis and Keller deliver the truth of Christianity to today's ever-chang-
ing culture, distilling the essentials of the faith down to their essence. They
are apologists who clear the path in a field of difficult questions, focusing on
the truth of the faith and who Christ is rather than wading through the tan-
gled debates of theology, infant or believer baptism, or which musical style is
appropriate for a church service. Those arguments are saved for the church
classrooms; the greatest concerns are the bigger issues like the problem of
evil, what aligns with Scripture, and who Jesus is.

Reading *Mere Christianity* and *The Reason for God* moves the academic,
rote church discussion into the realm of an honest and transparent conversation. The authors' style hearkens back to a time spent with a friend at the
neighborhood pub or café. Each author seems to lean across his armchair,
look you in the eye, and answer your burning, foundational questions about
the Christian faith. Why are evil and suffering in the world? How can I claim
that Christianity is the only true religion? I believed in the claims of my faith,
but *why*?

Both authors are featured in the C.S. Lewis Institute's Fellows program,[8]
where I first read Keller's *The Reason for God: Belief in an Age of Skepticism*.
As I studied the chapters, his words were like a parallel reading through my
favorite Lewis books because I found the same questions and that "pub talk"
accessibility I was searching for. In "Answers to Questions on Christianity"
from *God in the Dock*, Lewis was asked, "Supposing a factory worker asked
you: 'How can I find God?' How would you reply?"[9] Sixty years later, Keller
includes a similar question in his book when a scientist asks, "I can't believe
unless I find at least one absolutely airtight proof for God."[10]

These authors have an imaginative way of distilling the goodness, truth, and beauty of the faith.

Our faith is a journey stretching along a spiritual timeline. There is a starting point, and from that moment we struggle and rejoice as we learn more of what it means to follow Christ. There are as many sojourners as there are journeys, and somewhere along the way, we find a fellow Christian who speaks into our heart and soul with words that resonate.

I began my writing and work as a cultural apologist with a simple thought: I believe in God, but why? I wondered how I could adequately comfort someone who is crawling through a personal tragedy. And on the other hand, how can I bear witness to creation, beauty, and miracles that cannot be explained away with a simple formula or scientific theory? My journey with C.S. Lewis began many years ago. I was a marginal Christian at that time—still attending church, but only scratching the veneer of the faith. An acquaintance of mine at that time was digging into theology and had a copy of *Mere Christianity*. He told me to read through it and give him some feedback.

George Marsden shares that "As someone known for smoking and drinking, Lewis did not quite fit the American evangelical mold."[11] Many of us inside the church do seem to fit that American evangelical mold, which others who may want to attend. That is why the church must consciously reach out to and connect with a theologically disconnected world that is opening itself up to the most basic of questions.

This, of course, does not mean compromising the foundation of the Christian faith. Tim Keller set out to "begin a new church for a largely non-church-going population."[12] The idea was ridiculed, especially when he said that "the beliefs of the new church would be in the orthodox, historic tenets of Christianity—the infallibility of the Bible, the deity of Christ, the necessity of spiritual regeneration (the new birth)—all doctrines considered hopelessly dated by the majority of New Yorkers."[13] But decades later, thousands of new attendees continue to attend, perhaps because of the "intellectually grounded but non-inferential awareness of the divine"[14]—the *sensus divinitatis*—that is built into each of us.

Each of us has a worldview—a set of beliefs and attitudes that govern our interactions with other people and society. Your worldview may have adjusted over time, but when did you last ask yourself, "Why do I believe what I believe?" Introspection like this can be a bit jarring. You have come this far in life, functioning under a certain belief system, but stop and consider why. Tim Keller reminds us that "People who blithely go through life too busy or indifferent to ask hard questions about why they believe as they do will find themselves defenseless against either the experience of tragedy or the probing questions of a smart skeptic."[15]

Modern life has become like an old house and we are metaphorically painting layer upon layer of noise, lists, and goals with obligation and anger and desperation, choking out and covering up the goodness of God and the beauty of how we were created. These layers bury our sense of awe and wonder, but that glimmer of the holy is still there in each person. While the world becomes more splintered, people still crave unchanging truth.

The task of the church is to peel away the thick layers of the temporary and meaningless and begin again at the foundation to find the eternal. We will find that truth in the unadorned, unchanging word of God, who meets each of us through His plain-spoken disciples. As Saint Paul spoke to both Jew and Gentile, the church can reach those searching hearts through the words uniquely familiar and meaningful to them, just as Lewis spoke to the British soldiers and Keller shared with the young skeptics who came to Redeemer Presbyterian.

I recently experienced this same sort of spiritual generosity at a nearby Trappist monastery in the rolling hills of Virginia. My day-long pilgrimage was to be a reset for my scattered and discouraged mind. The purpose was to pray through the Liturgy of the Hours with the brothers as well as spend the day in silence, walking the grounds, and sitting in the chapel. After 7:00 a.m. Lauds, the monks filed out and I was alone in the simple chapel, surrounded by peace and waiting on the presence of God. The cycle continued through the day; the monastery bell would toll at the specific hours of the liturgy, and the brothers would enter the small chapel to chant and pray, then leave to other work.

One elderly monk stepped out of the procession and came to my pew to sit with me. My first thought was that I must have appeared out of place. I'm not Catholic, so I didn't share in the Eucharist during the first mass with the others who attended at 7:00 a.m. I couldn't find the right page in the liturgy booklet. I didn't know when to stand, kneel, or sit. Despite attending church all of my life, I felt awkward. This brother didn't see any of that—he just looked me in the eye and asked, "What brings you to us today?" (This act was no small matter. These Cistercian brothers take a vow of silence).

I told him that I came to pray all day and spend time with God alone. He held the fingers of his right hand to his thumb and tapped over his heart and said, "There is no space between you and God. He's here! Right here. There is a place in your heart that no evil can touch, like a diamond that no evil can enter. And that is where God lives."

He spoke with such sincerity that I knew he listened with a compassionate heart, speaking the only words I needed at that moment. This kind brother transcended religious denomination and time with his words to me. As we talked, he demonstrated generosity, kindness, and understanding. He handed me a prayer card and told me to keep it to read whenever I needed to be reminded that God was with me. I still carry this card in my notebook.

> My Lord God, I have no idea where I am going. I do not see the road ahead of me. I cannot know for certain where it will end. Nor do I really know myself, and the fact that I think that I am following your will does not mean that I am actually doing so. But I believe that the desire to please you does in fact please you. And I hope I have that desire in all that I am doing. I hope that I will never do anything apart from that desire. And I know that if I do this you will lead me by the right road though I may know nothing about it. Therefore I will trust you always though I may seem to be lost and in the shadow of death. I will not fear, for you are ever with me, and you will never leave me to face my perils alone.[16]

He openly spoke to my doubt that day, just like C.S. Lewis and Tim Keller: not with disregard, lectures, or tracts, but by recognizing my struggle in ordinary language. Questions do not change, but neither does truth. There are times when we must humbly admit that we have no answer, at least at the time of questioning. Admitting that we do not have an answer demonstrates an intellectual transparency that we are often loath to show.

Ultimately, it is the good purpose of apologists to dialogue with our increasingly secular culture about the basic questions of the Christian faith. We must be mindful of the prejudices that most of us carry into any religious debate. Arguing the fine points of a free-form approach of worship compared to liturgical tradition really only makes a difference to those who are in the church. We must step back from our positions and listen to the person who takes issue with moral law—that is where we should focus. In the Preface to *Christian Reflections*, Walter Hooper writes,

> Shortly after his conversion in 1929, C.S. Lewis wrote to a friend: "When all is said (and truly said) about the divisions of Christendom, there remains, by God's mercy, an enormous common ground." From

that time on Lewis thought that the best service he could do for his
unbelieving neighbours was to explain and defend the belief that has
been common to nearly all Christians at all times—that 'enormous
common ground; which he usually referred to as 'mere' Christianity."[17]

This common ground has not changed over a millenia and more. Humanity still looks to the stars and wonders how those flashing points of light
remain in constellations, unchanged over thousands of years. We watch the
bees on the flowers and marvel at the purpose of each, and the lavish beauty
of both. There is a reason why thousands of people continue to flock to Redeemer Presbyterian and its daughter churches, and why they continue to
buy copies of *Mere Christianity* and *The Reason for God.* The world wants to
dialogue, not to receive a mysterious message and a pat on the head and be
told to just believe. People want to be carefully considered.

The continued popularity of *Mere Christianity* and *The Reason for God* is
founded on the transcendent and timeless truths written in an "everyman"
voice that most readers can relate to and understand. Lewis states in his preface to *Mere Christianity* that "I am not writing to expound something I could
call 'my religion,' but to expound 'mere' Christianity, which is what it is and
what it was long before I was born and whether I like it or not."[18] Keller encourages the reader to also consider ideas of Christianity from skepticism,
asking "How do you know your belief is true?"[19] which is the basic question
common to theological and secular beliefs. The ideas of both authors are
presented as a practical conversation, not a debate, and conversations grow
out of relationship, the very thing that our society is missing.

Academics and philosophical studies in the field of Christian theology
are important, but never underestimate the power of a plain-spoken man
to reach the person who needs the simple message. These two authors ex-
emplify how to connect with our theologically fragmented culture, reaching
people in a rational and imaginative way. In *The Reason for God,* Tim Keller
demonstrates the heart of reaching out with the magnanimity and love of
Christ. Of C.S. Lewis, *Time* magazine said that "few 20th century men better understood the questions, or put the facts so well," and quoted Lewis in
their tribute to him: "All I'm doing," [Lewis] once told a BBC audience, "is to
get people to face the facts—to understand the questions which Christianity
claims to answer."[20] This is the work of both Keller and Lewis , and to them
both we are grateful.

ENDNOTES

1   C.S. Lewis, *Present Concerns: Journalistic Essays* (New York: HarperCollins, 1986), viii.

2   William Shakespeare, *Hamlet,* Act 2, Scene 2.

3   C.S. Lewis, *Mere Christianity* (New York: HarperCollins, 2001, orig. pub. 1952), x.

4   Lewis, *Mere Christianity,* vii.

5   George Marsden, "A Biography of Mere Christianity," *Knowing and Doing—C.S. Lewis Institute,* Spring 2017, https://www.cslewisinstitute.org/webfm_send/5791.

6   Timothy Keller, *The Reason for God: Belief in an Age of Skepticism* (New York: Riverhead Books, 2008), xxi.

7   For Keller's confirmation of the influence of C.S. Lewis's writing on his own ministry, please watch the video interview with John Piper at *Desiring God,* "Tim Keller and John Piper Discuss the Influence of C.S. Lewis," July 18, 2013, https://www.youtube.com/watch?v=4b5lXt9rqIQ.

8   For more information about the C.S. Lewis Institute and its Fellows program, go to https://www.cslewisinstitute.org/.

9   C.S. Lewis, "Answers to Questions on Christianity," in *God in the Dock: Essays on Theology and Ethics* (Grand Rapids, MI: Wm. B. Eerdmans, 1970), 38.

10   Keller, *Reason for God,* 130+.

11   Marsden, "Biography of *Mere Christianity.*"

12   Keller, *Reason for God,* xiv.

13   Ibid.

14   Brian Morley, *Mapping Apologetics: Comparing Contemporary Approaches* (Downer's Grove, IL: Inter-Varsity Press, 2015), 119.

15   Keller, *Reason for God,* xvii.

16   Thomas Merton, *Thoughts in Solitude* (New York: Farrar, Straus and Giroux, 1956), 79.

17   C.S. Lewis, *Christian Reflections* (Grand Rapids, MI: Wm. B. Eerdmans, 1967), vii.

18   Lewis, *Mere Christianity,* ix.

19   Keller, *Reason for God,* xix.

20   *Time* magazine wrote this tribute to C.S. Lewis a week after he died. The column included information on his work as a lecturer and professor, as well as discussion of his books. *Time* stated that "the Church of England has always been blessed with divines who could write of their faith with clarity, balance, style and, sometimes, with humor as well. Lewis—a layman who never took orders or a seminary course—had all these qualities in full measure" ("Theologians: Defender of the Faith," *Time* magazine, December 6, 1963, http://content.time.com/time/subscriber/article/0,33009,898102,00.html).

DENIS **HAACK**

Accessibility

FOLLOWERS OF JESUS AS BORDER-STALKERS

I've attended church regularly since childhood. This means I have heard—with wildly varying degrees of interest—approximately four thousand sermons over the course of my lifetime. (Many more than that if you factor in the ones given at summer church camps, weeknight meetings, retreats, conferences, and seminars.) And always there's been an expectation that I should invite non-Christian friends to attend with me. Almost never have I felt free to do so. A major reason is the sermon.

My problem was not that I've been afraid the truth would not be preached. I was usually confident it would be. The problem is that I was also confident the truth would be preached in language in which my friends were not conversant, and in categories that were of interest only to those that have already bought into the tribe that is the church.

It's a tribal problem. And that makes it difficult to address, because the same sermon that is inaccessible to the outsider may bless the socks off the members of the tribe.

The dialect of my tribe is my natural language. The categories of belief, feeling, and practice of my tribe are how I naturally tend to think, sense, and live. But preaching in this tribal dialect, using these tribal categories, erects a wall for the outsider. Because they are members of another tribe, they naturally speak another dialect and comprehend reality in different categories. "It is hard to overstate," Timothy Keller says, "how ghettoized our preaching is."[1]

The problem of cross-tribal communication is of course not unique to the church. It's not a religious issue; it's a fact of life in a pluralistic world. The problem becomes obvious when different languages are involved. If someone preaches in Xhosa in my Anglican church in Minnesota, no one will be surprised by the failure of communication. It's more surprising when fellow English speakers fail to comprehend one another because they speak

as members of differing tribes. Truth spoken in a common language may not
be heard and understood as truth if tribal dialects and categories intervene.

We all are members of some tribe—usually multiple tribes—where tribal
dialects and categories of thought that are so natural to those inside effectively keep outsiders outside. We become aware of the walls not by the ones
our tribe erects but by the ones built by others. These make us outsiders and
so are noticeable because they cause us discomfort. We've all been at par-
ties where people are talking animatedly about stuff we cannot comprehend
and about which we are distinctly uninterested. Comedy routines celebrate
the confusion and misunderstanding that occur at such walls. We want our
physician to drop his tribal dialect—no matter how useful it is for communicating with his fellow medical practitioners—and talk to us about our diagnosis in a way we can comprehend. We recognize instinctively that it's the
speaker's responsibility to bridge this vital gap.

For the church, this problem assumes added significance. Our gospel is
not just for us but for all. Our preaching should be understandable not just to
church members but to our non-Christian neighbors as well. Sadly, as Christian faith has become increasingly unattractive in our world of advanced
modernity, this communication gap has expanded into a looming chasm. My
grandfather grew up in a small town not far from where I live. His neighbor
would likely have understood a sermon about Jesus bearing the wrath of the
Father on the cross, even if he rejected the call to believe. But my neighbor
would likely be deeply offended by what she hears as an instance of divine
child abuse and may see my faith as containing dark and dangerous under-
currents of unjust relational cruelty.

And that brings me to what I see demonstrated so faithfully by Timothy
Keller. If the followers of Jesus are to be faithful to our Lord, our preaching
and witness must not merely be in words echoing within the walls of our
tribe. We need to walk past our tribe's walls to visit, listen, befriend, serve, and
learn in the spaces where members of different tribes mingle. In other words,
the followers of Jesus need to become skilled, intentional *mearcstapa*—
border-stalkers.

Borrowing an idea from *Beowulf* and Tolkien, Makoto Fujimura likens
the artist to a border-stalker. "They cross tribal norms to see the whole, to
navigate between the walls erected to protect the tribes," he says. Fujimura
believes artists adopt this role naturally because of the nature of their calling,
and argues it is not only admirable but essential. "Border-stalkers have the
ability to learn and communicate extratribal languages" and "are increas-

ingly valued in cultures that are polarized."[2] They "lower barriers to understanding and communication, and start to defuse the culture wars."[3]

Keller is a preacher, not an artist in the sense Fujimura is considering, but he is a creative border-stalker. And this at a time when many preachers—indeed, many Christians—are busy reinforcing the walls of their tribe in a culture war in which they feel under assault by the majority society, by the tribes outside their walls. In his preaching, and by extension in his writing, Keller seeks instead to imaginatively speak in terms that non-Christians can engage with. He has listened to his non-Christian neighbors carefully enough to learn their language and identify how the yearnings of their hearts are unmet by the reductionistic secularism of their world. He communicates the gospel in this context in a way they can understand and appreciate. Christians listening to his preaching are thus shown week by week an example of how they might bridge the gap so that those outside the church might apprehend the story of the gospel. In this he demonstrates the accessibility of the gospel in both preaching and witness.

My wife and I became aware of Timothy Keller around the time Redeemer Presbyterian was launched in 1989. The scuttlebutt in the Presbyterian Church in America, of which we were members, was that Keller was a preacher worth hearing, and the growth of Redeemer in secular, hostile Manhattan was impressive. We had friends that began attending Redeemer and reported that they would happily invite any non-Christian friend, no matter how skeptical or hostile, to attend if Keller was preaching. He preached to the church full of Christians but spoke in terms that made sense to non-Christians, presenting a gospel of grace without watering it down. Rather than shy away from hard topics and texts, he addressed them, and did so in ways that made people think in fresh ways. His authenticity was easily apparent, and though his learning was impressive he was never elitist or pedantic.

We knew precious few followers of Jesus who would say this about their own church and pastor's preaching. The concerns addressed by many sermons are often not the concerns of our neighbors, or if they are, they are expressed in terms that do not resonate with how our neighbors ordinarily think and live. Many sermons give the impression that Christian faith is a private affair and has little of substance to say to those outside the tribe's walls.

We were already considering these issues because two decades earlier a crisis of faith had been resolved under the influence of Edith and Francis Schaeffer. We saw the same dynamic at work in them. They proclaimed the gospel of grace, tackling hard topics but always in ways that drew non-Christians into ongoing conversation rather than ending the discussion. Regardless of the biblical text under consideration, its themes were brought into creative tension with the thinking and practice of the wider culture, the world outside the church's walls. They believed that Jesus Christ is Lord of all, which meant that Christianity had something intelligent and substantial to say to every aspect of life, culture, and reality. They understood the doctrines of the faith as addressing the perennial questions of humankind, and they placed the story of Scripture in tension with our personal story. The Schaeffers mentioned movies not as illustrations of a point but as essential parts of an ongoing cultural conversation about things that matter. They took non-Christian thinkers seriously, appreciating their insights while showing that their worldview was incomplete apart from Christ, just as Saint Paul did in Athens (Acts 17). The Schaeffers spoke in the vernacular, and as a result L'Abri attracted scores of people who would never darken the door of a church. Long before we were introduced to the terms, *missional* and *border-stalking* had become essential aspects of our Christian faithfulness.

Keller has been intentional about speaking in the vernacular from the beginning of his ministry in New York. In his 2001 article "The Missional Church," for example, he identified the need to "speak in the vernacular" as one of the nonnegotiable "practices of the missional church."

> In Christendom there is little difference between the language inside and outside of the church; technical biblical terms are well known inside and outside church life. Documents of the early US Congress, for example, are riddled with allusions to and references from the Bible. In a missional church, however, these terms must be explained.
> The missional church:
> - avoids "tribal" language, stylized prayer language, unnecessarily pious evangelical jargon, and archaic language that seeks to set a spiritual tone.
> - avoids "we-they" language, disdainful jokes that mock people of different politics and beliefs, and dismissive, disrespectful comments about those who differ with us.
> - avoids sentimental, pompous, "inspirational" talk.
> - avoids talking as if nonbelieving people were not present. If you speak and discourse as if your whole neighborhood were present (and not just scattered Christians), eventually more and more of your neighbors will find their way in or be invited.

Unless all of the above is the outflow of a truly humble-bold, gospel-changed heart, it is all just marketing and spin.[4]

And in his article "Evangelistic Worship," Keller sharply critiques evangelical preaching.

It is hard to overstate how ghettoized our preaching is. It is common to make all kinds of statements that appear persuasive to us but are based upon all sorts of premises that the secular person does not hold; it is common to use terms and phrases that mean nothing outside of our Christian subgroup. So avoid unnecessary theological or evangelical subculture jargon, and explain carefully the basic theological concepts—confession of sin, praise, thanksgiving, and so on. In the preaching, show continual willingness to address the questions that the unbelieving heart will ask. Speak respectfully and sympathetically to people who have difficulty with Christianity. As you write the sermon, imagine a particular skeptical non-Christian in the chair listening to you. Add the necessary asides, the definitions, the extra explanations. Listen to everything said in the worship service with the ears of someone who has doubts or troubles with belief.[5]

And he urges preachers to speak directly to the concerns of non-Christians in categories and terms they themselves employ.

Speak regularly to "those of you who aren't sure you believe this, or who aren't sure just what you believe." Give them many asides, even employing the language of their hearts. Articulate their objections to Christian living and belief better than they can do it themselves. Express sincere sympathy for their difficulties, even when challenging them severely for their selfishness and unbelief. Admonish with tears (literally or figuratively). Always grant whatever degree of merit their objections have. It is extremely important that unbelievers feel you understand their objections: "I've tried it before and it did not work." "I don't see how my life could be the result of the plan of a loving God." "Christianity is a straitjacket." "It can't be wrong if it feels so right." "I could never keep it up." "I don't feel worthy; I am too bad." "I just can't believe."

As a layman I have relatively few opportunities to apply Keller's example of accessibility in my preaching. Over the years, however, Margie and I have tried to creatively demonstrate it and to train the followers of Jesus in the same skills. We're convinced that each follower of Jesus must learn to be and have the courage to become *mearcstapa.*

The first way we've attempted to do this is by emphasizing *learning to listen.*

We've begun this training not in the borderlands, but in a setting where Christians feel very much at home: in small group Bible study. Our experience is that Evangelicals tend to dive immediately into Interpretation—saying what they think the text means or what they've heard some pastor or theologian say it means. In doing this they are skipping over the first crucial step of Bible study, which is careful Observation of the text itself. Interpretation seems more critical and is often more exciting than taking the time to read and observe the details carefully, and then to observe some more. Noting the details of the text and the flow of the narrative is of course essential to proper interpretation, but it's easy to assume we know what the Scripture says after reading it aloud together. Besides, many of us have heard the text before, perhaps many times. So, to counter this tendency, we've emphasized the need to observe, carefully and without hurrying, insisting that no interpretation occur until we've spent significant time observing what's in the text and its context. Observation is taking time to listen to the text. Occasionally, when we find the members slide back into bad patterns of interpreting first, we'll announce that in this meeting all we'll do is read the text and observe, saving Analysis (Interpretation) and Response (Application) for the next meeting.[6] We think learning to listen is that important. Over time most study members come to agree with us.

We also quietly but firmly insist during the discussion that comments begin with specific observations, whether it is some detail in the text or some aspect of the biblical story we are studying. This keeps the discussion from veering off into mere opinion—there will be plenty of time for sharing such things when we get to the end and talk about how we are responding to the Scripture. It's been interesting that non-Christians who become part of our Bible studies have been particularly appreciative of this emphasis on carefully listening to the text. When someone ventures an opinion unrelated to any observation, we gently ask, "Where did you see that in the text?" It's not been uncommon for our non-Christian friends to ask that once they feel safe with us in the group. "Let's talk about the text," they'll insist when the speaker admits it was just something they were thinking about, "we're here to study this text."

We've emphasized Observation in Bible study because we want our group members to be truly listening to the Scriptures. And we've emphasized this Bible study skill because listening is a crucial border-stalker skill.

Second, we also introduce, in our Bible study training, *Response questions that explicitly prepare members for the borderlands,* for cross-tribal communication, for discourse in the vernacular.

It has been our experience that Evangelicals tend to be handicapped when it comes to the final step of inductive Bible study, Respond (Apply). The tendency is to reduce it to, "What does this text mean to me?" We must actively resist this for several reasons, the one most relevant here being that it implicitly reinforces a ghetto mindset and worldview. Besides undercutting the Lordship of Christ across all of life, culture, and reality, it invites a subjective sense of comfort within the walls of the tribe.

So, we've posed Response questions such as:

- How can we speak of the truth(s) we've learned in this text so that our non-Christian neighbors might understand and be intrigued?
- How can we creatively summarize this text/story of Scripture in a way that might be attractive to our non-Christian neighbors, that will perhaps continue the conversation rather than end it?
- If a non-Christian friend or colleague asks what you did last night, what could you say from this text that might cause them to be interested?
- What categories of concern—which of the perennial yearnings of the human heart—are addressed in this text?

Christians have often told us this was initially the most challenging and difficult part of our Bible studies. In raising these questions we've often asked the group to reflect on how to raise questions that probe the text we are studying. This is a subset skill of listening and crucial to border-stalking.

It takes time and patience to demonstrate that even the "religious" or "spiritual" topics addressed in the biblical text can be set in a context understandable by those outside, including those that are hostile to the faith. For example, most people yearn for some sense of meaning and purpose in life.

When discussing biblical texts on calling and mission, we can place them in the context of this yearning. Another example is expressing gratitude. Recent articles on the problem of languishing due to the COVID pandemic suggest expressing gratitude as a partial cure.[7] This can be part of the context of a sermon or conversation on worship.

Whenever we are discussing texts that address the deepest yearnings of humankind, we can demonstrate how the four-stanza story of Scripture addresses the deepest yearning of the human heart, expressed in the big questions posed throughout human history.

CREATION
- What is really real—the ultimate nature of reality?
- Is there a God? If yes, what is he/she/it like?
  If no, what does that imply?
- What does it mean to be human?
- Where are we?

FALL
- Why is there suffering and death?
- How do we know what is good and what is evil?
- Why is the "Perfect" always out of reach?
- What went wrong? Why?

REDEMPTION
- What's the solution to what went wrong?
- Is there an answer to suffering and death?
- What happens at death?
- Can evil and injustice be redeemed?

NEW CREATION
- What's the meaning of life? Of my life?
- What's the purpose of history?
- How will things end?
- Is there reason to hope?

And, as Keller proposes, "at the opportune time, point to the unsurpassed resources of Christianity for each":

- A meaning in life that suffering can't take away,
  but can even *deepen*
- A satisfaction that isn't based on circumstances
- A freedom that doesn't reduce community and
  relationships to thin transactions
- An identity that isn't fragile or based on our performance
  or the exclusion of others
- A way to both deal with guilt and forgive others without
  residual bitterness or shame
- A basis for seeking justice that does not turn us into
  oppressors ourselves
- A way to face not only the future, but death itself with
  poise and peace
- An explanation for the senses of transcendent beauty
  and love we often experience[8]

Our preaching needs to make these connections so that Christian belief and practice is seen as addressing the human condition in a fallen world. And in Bible study we can teach laypeople to listen objectively, ask probing questions, and intentionally relate the faith to all of life.

A third thing we have done is intentionally bring significant *artifacts from the borderlands* into our Bible studies.

We've interspersed our evenings of Bible study with discussions of short stories, poetry, music, and movies. We've also encouraged members to bring to the group memos, papers, syllabi, videos, or other materials that are used for training or address values used in their place of work. About every six weeks we host a group meeting devoted to reflecting on and discussing this material, using the same basic study skills the group has learned. We've encouraged listening carefully—being certain we hear correctly and accurately before responding. We've asked the group to imagine the material's principal author, director, etc., is present. The goal must be that after we've listened and observed, the author would we've heard them correctly and well, regardless of whether we go on to disagree in part or in whole.

We've imagined these times as exercises in border-stalking, bringing something of value from a neighboring tribe to our tribe to learn their language and categories. This provides Christians with the opportunity to learn how to appeal to thinkers and stories, as Saint Paul did in Athens, that are significant in the wider culture instead of merely in the Sunday school classroom.

The exercises have proved to the non-Christians in our group that we are taking them seriously and that the group is a safe place for them to explore their ideas, beliefs, and values. And we've intended, through these exercises, to train Christians to be border-stalkers, who will hopefully become more fluent in the dialect of neighboring tribes.

And finally, we draw all this together by teaching what we refer to as the *process of Christian discernment.*

We've argued that rather than being reactionary in a fallen world, the followers of Jesus need to be discerning. Discernment is simple enough to teach to children but profound enough to guide us as we reflect on the most difficult and complex issues that come our way. The process can be summarized in a series of reflection and discussion questions. We've used this series of questions repeatedly in discussions of all sorts of artifacts from the borderlands. Becoming conversant in these skills prepares us to use them effectively when we are suddenly faced with a decision or question which we have not considered. And, of course, we've insisted that the discerning Christian is comfortable saying, "I don't know, but I'll try to find out."

The process of discernment includes six reflection questions:

- What's being communicated? What story is being told?
- What's made to be attractive/unattractive? How?
- Where do I agree, and why?
- What should I question or challenge, and why?
- How can I speak about and flesh out what I believe winsomely and creatively in a pluralistic world?

These questions, with a bit of tweaking for the genre being considered, can be used to discuss a movie or a short story, unpack an op-ed piece, bring us into a new music recording, or help guide us as we reflect on some challenge posed by a colleague at work.

We have commended this process as the basic skill set required of a border-stalker—even though we have seldom used that term. By regularly practicing these skills in the safety of our Bible study, we prepare ourselves for life outside the walls of our tribe. These discernment skills also parallel inductive Bible study skills.[9] This allows us to reinforce both skill sets regardless of the specific agenda for our discussion on any particular evening. Our prayer is that these skills and border-land exercises will translate into a lifestyle of faithfulness.

The world we live in is highly politicized, and ideologies commend themselves to the people of God as modern idolatries.[10] Many Christians have allowed a commitment to some ideology or agenda to become primary in their hearts, failing to recognize how their faith has been compromised. This is parallel to the Baal worship that seduced the Old Testament people of God, the spiritual adultery that is always a danger in a fallen world. This means that not only is discernment and serious Bible study necessary for the church, but we can also expect pushback when believers discover that their values, priorities, and practices are less than fully orthodox.

Fujimura recognizes that the task of the border-stalker often involves discord, skepticism, and misunderstanding. The borderlands are dangerous, and border-stalkers are usually viewed with suspicion by both the neighboring tribe and their own.

> *Mearcstapa* is not a comfortable role. Life on the borders of a group—and in the space between groups—is prone to dangers literal and figurative, with people both at "home" and among the "other" likely to misunderstand or mistrust the motivations, piety and loyalty of the border-stalker. But *mearcstapa* can be a role of cultural leadership in a new mode, serving functions including empathy, memory, warning, guidance, mediation, and reconciliation. Those who journey to the borders of their group and beyond will encounter new vistas and knowledge that can enrich the group.[11]

It always feels safest within the walls. Border-stalking, in sharp contrast, takes courage, requires a willingness to chart new paths, and consistently produces disequilibrium. It requires safe people to walk boldly and humbly into unsafe territory. It's part of picking up our cross and following Christ into the borderlands of our world. In other words, it's a necessary radicalism for Christian faithfulness in the twenty-first century West. Christians need to learn how to accomplish it, and preachers can demonstrate what it looks like in their sermons.

By God's grace may it be so.

Holy Father, you have revealed yourself in creation (the word made), Scripture (the word written), and supremely in Christ (the living Word). May your people be faithful border-stalkers. May we learn to speak of your grace winsomely and demonstrate it through sacrificial service in love in our skeptical world in ways that cause conversations about the things that matter most to flourish rather than end, doing the hard work to translate the gospel into terms and categories that our non-Christian neighbors might apprehend, by the power of the Holy Spirit and to the glory of your Son, who with You reign as One God, world without end. Amen.

ENDNOTES

1   Tim Keller, "Evangelistic Worship," *Redeemer City to City,* January 1, 2001, https://redeemercitytocity.com/articles-stories/evangelistic-worship.

2   Makoto Fujimura, *Art + Faith: A Theology of Making* (New Haven, CT: Yale University Press, 2020), 15, 46.

3   Makoto Fujimura, *Culture Care: Reconnecting with Beauty for Our Common Life* (Downers Grove, IL: IVP Books, 2017), 39.

4   Tim Keller, "The Missional Church," *Redeemer City to City,* January 1, 2001, https://redeemercitytocity.com/articles-stories/the-missional-church.

5   Keller, "Evangelistic Worship."

6   We use the terms Analyze for Interpret and Respond for Apply because they appeared less "churchy" and so more acceptable to the skeptical Christians and non-Christians that joined our studies. Though this is only a guess, we think this may also be related to the wide acceptance of the method of natural science as a neutral process for discovering truth. When Survey is added at the beginning, to identify details of dating, genre, and the like, the acronym for the entire process is SOAR. Easy to teach and remember.

7   I comment on two such pieces on our website in "From Languishing to Flourishing" (*Critique Letters,* accessed February 1, 2022, https://www.critique-letters.com/from-languishing-to-flourishing/).

8   Timothy Keller, *How to Reach the West Again: Six Essential Elements of a Missionary Encounter* (New York: Redeemer City to City, 2020). A free copy is available online: https://redeemercitytocity.com/reachthewest.

9   Both are expressions of SOAR:

INDUCTIVE STUDY	PROCESS OF DISCERNMENT
Survey/Observation	What's being said?
Analyze	What's made attractive?
	Where do I agree, and why?
	What would I question/challenge, and why?
Respond	How can I speak about and flesh out the truth winsomely in a pluralistic world?

10 David Koyzis, *Political Visions & Illusions: A Survey and Christian Critique of Contemporary Ideologies* (Downers Grove, IL: InterVarsity Press, 2003).

11 Fujimura, *Culture Care,* 40.

J. MARK **BERTRAND**

Influence

GOSPEL IN THE PUBLIC SQUARE

My wife has a framed photo of Tim Keller on her desk, a white elephant gift that has long outlived the intended irony and remained so long in residence that I finally had to unearth a picture of myself as a counterweight. I set it beside Tim's, my frame overlapping his ever so slightly.

The reason she was given that gift—and the reason it stuck around so long—is that Tim Keller is my wife's favorite pastor. She has told me this repeatedly, though there was no need to spell it out. I can't count the number of times I've heard her on the phone dispensing Keller sermons to friends in crisis the way other church ladies prescribe essential oils. "You need to listen to 'The Struggle for Love,'" she'll say, "and then we'll discuss it." Or, "I think you'd better go back to 'Lord of the Wine.'" Or she'll call me over to listen to a clip from the lecture series Keller did with Edmund Clowney on preaching in a postmodern context, some bit of advice or insight she thinks I need to hear. As I said, Keller is her favorite pastor.

Perhaps I should mention that I am a pastor, too.

But I came late to the calling as one untimely born, and I accept the precedence gratefully because I, too, have been influenced by Tim Keller.

His way of orienting the gospel toward the life of the city breathed hope into my own call to contribute to that life. As a product of the anti-intellectual strain of Christianity, my awakening to the faith had progressed hand in hand with a talent for cultural criticism. But my ambition was to write novels, and for that more than a critical gaze was required. I'd gone to seminary after finishing my MFA in creative writing in search of a positive theological vision to inform my creative work. Like Jacob and the angel, I had a way of wrestling with professors in search of a blessing, only to discover how much of a silo theological knowledge can be. Sometimes the guide can tell you only that you were made in the image of the Creator, because he has never had occasion to ask what that might mean for your own creative work. But eventually my quest led me to Keller, and if all my questions were not immediately resolved, at least I knew that I was asking in the right place.

When I found myself, later, dragged reluctantly into the task of church planting, I stumbled forward with a dog-eared copy of the Redeemer church-planting handbook, deciphering as best I could what the mysterious charts might mean, so that later I could laugh at anyone who found *Center Church* a challenge to digest. I led a core group through the video curriculum for *The Reason for God,* marveling that instead of filming himself on stage before a friendly audience, Keller assembled a panel of unconvinced interlocutors to challenge him on each point, which he then answered with disarming grace. And I have prescribed Keller's books in much the same way my wife has his sermons. Struggling in your relationship? Here, take *The Meaning of Marriage.* Worried about the state of your piety? Here, take *Prayer: Experiencing Awe and Intimacy with God.*

All this to say that, yes, Tim Keller has influenced me, and influenced others through me. And yet that word—influence—is one I hoped to avoid in writing this, despite the fact that it is inescapably my theme.

I am ambivalent about "influence" because for me it is often a hedge. I own people as influences as a way of declining their names as a label. In an apologetics class, for example, I was once asked point blank whether I was a Van Tillian. Cornelius Van Til was famously obscure, so much so that his students developed a cottage industry interpreting what he meant. I have read enough of Van Til's work with sufficient appreciation to think that accepting the label might be justified, yet I cannot quite bring myself to do it. You may think it's over scrupulous, but I imagine myself claiming to be a Van Tillian only to have the man appear, specter-like, prompted by my invocation to insist that I depart from him, never having known him. I do not think I am alone in this. So instead of claiming the title, I only replied, "I have been influenced by him."

Another problem with claims of influence is how they signal aspiration. I made the mistake of answering honestly when my application for grad school asked about my literary influences: Shakespeare, Robert Ludlum, and Marcel Proust. This was the equivalent of falling into three traps all at once. If an influence is so ubiquitous that literally everyone has been shaped by it, as is the case with Shakespeare, then it hardly merits mention. All I accomplished by citing the Bard was to reveal the youthful alloy of my naïveté and delusions of grandeur. By the same token, if an influence is popular but not admirable, as Ludlum's was, you merely disclose a lack of taste. Even worse, if you've only read a few pages by one of your supposed influences—and I had only read a few pages of Proust at that time, the madeleine passage, which we roughly translated in my French lab—then your own work will show no evidence of it. I was a pretentious but lackluster acolyte.

Fortunately for me, that application was returned unread because I'd missed the deadline, and by the time I applied and was accepted, I'd had time to discover how thorny the question of influence can be. Sometimes it's a mask, sometimes it's a ploy, and inevitably the effort of self-scrutiny undoes a little of the magic, making it difficult to accept in the end that this writer, this work, this word really formed you to such an extent.

All this to say, I use the word influence with trepidation, wishing I could find a better way to put it, but I am convinced that when we celebrate Tim Keller, what we're celebrating is not a particular sermon he preached, not a book he wrote, not a class he taught, or even a church he planted. It is neither any one of these things in particular nor all of them taken together. Nor is it the rhetorical alchemy by which the sum is said to be greater than its parts. We do celebrate them, of course, and any one of them taken on its own terms would be worthy of celebration. But what we truly celebrate is *what has been accomplished in and through them,* and lacking a better word for that "what," I will call it influence.

Put it this way. At a banquet last year I was seated next to the young pastor of a nondenominational megachurch. He had no idea who I was, but hoping to help me along in my journey of faith, he leaned forward and said that the greatest influence on his own ministry was this Presbyterian pastor called Tim Keller. He confided this in a tone that suggested I might never have encountered that curious sect and would certainly never have heard of its most winsome contemporary exponent. I wanted to clasp him by the hand and tell him that I am in fact a minister in the same denomination, that Tim's photo sits framed on my wife's desk, only slightly eclipsed by my own. But instead I simply smiled. I have been on the giving end of that pitch so often, pressing Keller upon the unsuspecting, that finding myself on the receiving end is a delight. And again, it's a testament to an influence that has surged well beyond the banks. Call me a cynic, but a flood like this typically accompanies only the bad influences, whereas Keller's is anything but.

If I had to say what makes his influence such a good one, judging as a whole rather than taking it book-by-book or sermon-by sermon, my answer might seem idiosyncratic. It is certainly subjective. Yet I think there's something to this that will resonate with anyone who rediscovered the Reformed theological tradition, as I did, rather than inheriting it. There is a tendency when such riches are recovered to long for repristination, to feel that a wrong turn was taken by your forebears which can only be righted by going all the way back. Filled with awe by the old confessions, trembling with anticipation as you leaf through the pages of almost forgotten books, you want nothing more than to knock together a booth like Peter at the Transfiguration, a house to contain it all so that the glory might be beheld. Let's call it a museum, because the theology is so much treasure, so much art in the highest sense, and it feels that the best thing you could devote your life to is to gild a frame to set around the doctrine, underscoring its worth, and to throw a velvet rope across the threshold to keep anyone from getting close enough to touch.

This is the response of someone who's read a few pages of Calvin's *Institutes*, as I'd read a few pages of Proust. Read further and your sense of how to serve this material will change. Instead of keeping it cordoned behind the rope, you'll want to take it out into the world. You'll forget your Genevan nostalgia and want to turn the old insights loose in the contemporary world, no longer believing that they need to be protected from interference or innovation, because you've become convinced they can more than hold their own, that they have a contribution to make now, that the exit that takes us to the road less traveled might yet be accessible without having to retrace several centuries of steps.

Or to put it another way, when I want to encourage someone to read Calvin and form a judgment firsthand apart from hearsay, I'll recommend Marilynne Robinson's essay "Marguerite de Navarre" or her introduction to an anthology of the Reformer's writings. But if I wanted to demonstrate what it might look like for the spiritual and psychological insights of Calvin to live and breathe in the modern world, I would suggest the work—any work— of Tim Keller, who seems to me the best example of taking the inheritance and setting it loose in the public sphere. This is why I think his influence is so salutary: Keller makes this spiritual tradition accessible by showing not only that it speaks to questions we still ask ourselves today, but that it speaks with unique authority to those questions, offering not a way back but a way forward, if we have ears to hear.

My wife taught me this, to be honest.

I'd come into the kitchen before dinner with the first volume of the *Institutes,* reading page after page aloud, no doubt tempting her to put the knife in her hand to an unculinary use. When I paused for breath and invited comment on the passage I'd just read, she replied, "Well, yes … but the way Tim Keller would put it is like this." And she'd restate Calvin's labyrinthine insights into straightforward maxims straight out of the Keller oeuvre.

It almost became a bit of a challenge, me offering up passage after passage and her answering with faithful paraphrases, until I finally gave up on the idea of introducing her to anything new in Calvin, because she had already encountered him in a livelier form. While I'm not saying that Keller's influence can be summed up as simply a popularization of Calvin, I do think that Tim Keller as an idea, a phenomenon, rests somehow upon a sublimation of Calvin, and that his gift to us has been a demonstration of what the truth we value in common with him might look like when it is actually lived and put to use.

CITY

DAVID **BISGROVE**

Presence

JONAH AND THE BIG APPLE

"That's the dumbest idea I've ever heard."

Those may not be the exact words that came out of my mouth, but over the years it is the phrase that best captures my state of mind when a friend told me about a new church that was about to launch on the Upper East Side of Manhattan. Those words revealed both my Jonah-like view of God and New York City and the Abraham-like faith and courage of a husband and wife who left a comfortable life in the suburbs of Philadelphia to launch Redeemer Presbyterian Church. This is my attempt to honor the lives and legacy of Tim and Kathy's influence in my life and the lives of my fellow urban pilgrims who sought to live out God's vision of serving and loving this glorious city.

HERE TO STAY

When I first heard about this "crazy idea," I was already attending a church pastored by a gifted teacher with a national profile. Tim, on the other hand, was known only to a small circle inside the Presbyterian denomination with which he was affiliated. So why leave an established church just a few blocks from my apartment for a church that was more concept than reality? Surprisingly it wasn't the preaching but the impact of a phrase the Kellers uttered to a small gathering in their apartment: "We are here to stay." Until that moment I didn't realize how much I longed to hear those words, as I was just beginning to experience the relational exhaustion and isolation that comes from calling Manhattan home. Reflecting back on that evening I realize how those words reached into what James Baldwin called the "irrevocable condition" of home that we all carry inside of us. They met a longing for permanence and stability in my life at a time when most of what I saw around me was transience and relationships with shallow roots.

Given the impact of both Redeemer and its sister organization City to City it might seem like an obvious strategy to call Christians to root themselves in global cities. But it was no sure thing in 1989, as New York City was just beginning to emerge from a dark chapter, with few signs of the cultural and economic renaissance that would mark the following two decades. For example, the apartment in which I lived during my two years at graduate school was across the street from Bryant Park, which at the time was a haven for drug dealers peddling crack in plastic vials that crunched under my shoes as I made my way to the subway.

It was into that city that Tim and Kathy moved with their three young sons and became models of faithful presence. For the first decade of Redeemer's ministry Tim intentionally turned down opportunities to speak at national conferences, telling me one time he'd rather spend two hours with ten college students in Queens than speak before one thousand conference attendees in some other city. He was constantly meeting with small groups of Christians and seekers, whether at places like the Harvard Club on Friday mornings or with college students on Friday nights. For a few months I had the privilege of partnering with him in a ministry to a small community in Greenwich Village for whom evangelical Christianity was more a community of judgment than grace. We would sit around small tables with just a handful of people reading and discussing Scripture. The point is that Tim and Kathy lived out the text that is most associated with Redeemer's vision (Jer. 29:4–9), in which Christians are to see themselves as exiles called by God to love and seek the flourishing of the city.

It is a lot easier to talk and write about proximity, parish, and faithful presence than it is to live it out. The allure of blog posts, social media followers, podcasts, and book deals distracts many of us from the incarnational nature of pastoral ministry. And the well-documented social disconnection caused by technology, not to mention the simultaneous disruptions of the global pandemic, political polarization, and perspectives on race and justice have accelerated the commodification and consumerism of congregational engagement. This isn't a new challenge for the church. Saint Benedict added the vow of "stability" to the vows of chastity, poverty, and obedience to encourage the followers of Jesus to model Jesus' incarnation. This is not to say that blogs, social media, podcasts, and books aren't important, and technology has allowed our congregation to stay connected during the darkest days of the pandemic. But the orthopraxy that flowed from Tim and Kathy's orthodoxy is a timely reminder that there is no substitute for Christians staying in places like NYC, forming deep connections with one another while living side by side with people who find your faith strange and sometimes dangerous. This, after all, is what Jesus did.

SOME OF YOU ARE THINKING

I grew up in a wonderful church community that loved Jesus and each other and where the Bible was faithfully preached and taught. But as in many Christian spaces there was an unconscious assumption that everyone sitting in the pew agreed with the message. This kind of environment habituates Christians, like frogs in warming kettles, to lose the capacity to exercise a spiritual discipline that is key to formation, which is to doubt the very faith they claim to hold. In most churches, doubt and faith are presented as non-overlapping binaries. You either believe or you don't. Worship services, sermons, classes, and Bible studies are often crafted in a way that assumes the hearers are either unquestioning saints or lost sinners. So when I first heard Tim utter the phrase "Now I know some of you are thinking" in the middle of one of his sermons I could almost hear myself shout the words "Yes! How did you know?!" In other words, it was the first time in the context of something like worship that my doubts were given permission to come out of hiding into the light of the mystery of faith, allowing me to experience Frederich Buechner's insight that "doubts are the ants in the pants of faith. They keep it awake and moving."[1] Or as Tim put it in his book *Reason for God*:

> A faith without some doubts is like a human body with no antibodies in it… Only if you struggle long and hard with objections to your faith will you be able to provide the grounds for your beliefs to skeptics, including yourself, that are plausible rather than ridiculous or offensive.[2]

Living with the paradox found in the prayer "I believe; Help my unbelief!" (Mark 9:24) can be frightening at first, but Tim's constant infusion of those apologetic antibodies was a chance for an entire community of exiles to cross what theologian Kenneth Archer calls "the desert of skeptical criticism" together. We were a community shaped by the permission to doubt. This shared experience has two related impacts. First, admitting and exploring unbelief often leads to the humble realization that the possibility of leaving Jesus behind leads to the conclusion expressed by the Apostle Peter who, when asked by Jesus if the disciples were going to give in to their doubt and leave him as well, said: "To whom would we go? You have the words that give eternal life?" (John 6:68 NLT) This in turn allows for spiritual conversations with those inside and outside the church to be marked by humility and curiosity as opposed to certainty and dogmatism.

Tim and Kathy modeled this humility and curiosity, regularly reminding staff and leaders that every event at the church should be crafted in such a way that assumed the presence of unbelief. We were to imagine a co-worker, friend, or relative who was openly skeptical of Christianity sitting in the pew, classroom, or living room and shape our liturgy, content, and conversations accordingly. As many of you know this is not as easy as it might sound. In this moment, we see the destruction of every truth claim celebrated, while the existential disruption caused by the pandemic has caused so many people to question life's meaning. In the midst of this, the permission to doubt modeled by Tim and Kathy is as important as ever. Whether we face the rise of the *nones* (the religiously unaffiliated), the decreasing church engagement by Christians, or the dogmatic divisions inside the church, the Kellers' approach to doubt reminds us of the importance of combining the rigor of exploring the intellectual aspect of our doubts (*Making Sense of God*) with the discipline of practicing God's presence (*Walking with God Through Pain and Suffering*). In other words, doubt resides in both our heads and our hearts, and oftentimes what we and others need isn't just for our questions to be answered, but our pain to be seen. And it starts with giving yourself and others permission to doubt.

LOST IN THE WOODS

I spent the better part of two years traveling to Tim and Kathy's apartment to take seminary classes, the same apartment where I first heard the words "here to stay" and the place they still call home. The apartment is full of books, including a voluminous number of Puritan sermons and writings. One evening I remember a discussion about the amount of time it takes to explore and absorb the insights of the Puritans. Tim's response was that reading the Puritans was a lot like wandering into a dense and beautiful forest—one that lots of people enter, never to be seen again. In other words there is always a danger that deeply engaging in one particular theological tradition can cause you to miss out on a much wider world of theological reflection.

I share this because it represents something core to Tim's effectiveness, which is a curiosity of mind and heart that keeps him open to voices outside his theological tribe. Tim's humility and curiosity have enriched his preaching and writing and are some of the reasons he has been so effective in a place like NYC. They are also an antidote to the harmful sectarianism and polarization that currently faces the broader church. The rigidity and animus that marks much of Christian dialogue around subjects like politics and race is in part a consequence of pride and a lack of curiosity among Christians who are lost in the woods of their own streams. This is not to say that we at Redeemer or Tim discovered the perfect bread crumbs to lead us to some kind of Eden-like unity and theological creed. But it does open up a deeper understanding of God who is: both the Word made flesh and the mysterious Spirit who is like a rushing wind (Acts 2:1–2) that blows where He pleases (John 3:8).

The single most critical factor, however, that contributes to Tim's ability to speak to our culture with wisdom and authority is his love for and study of Scripture. He might be known for his capacity to read cultural tea leaves, to break down complicated philosophical and sociological positions and weave them into sermons and books, but if you have listened to his sermons over the years it is his fidelity to God's word and its core message of the good news of Jesus that remains the center of his reflections. In the late nineties we decided to create "Vision Groups" as a strategy to connect more people to one another through smaller communities. Part of the strategy was linking the sermon text to the weekly written study guides, which required Tim to write sermon notes for those responsible for creating the guides. Those single spaced, multi-page notes are brilliant and practical commentaries that reveal Tim's detailed exegesis of each text. They remain some of the most valuable resources for my own personal devotions and sermon preparation.

Yes, Tim has consumed thousands of pages of non-biblical material over the years, and it has informed his writing and preaching. But his reading of, and reflection on, the biblical text and story have always been and continue to be foundational to his contribution to the church. As he has said, in a world of cultural confusion there is no book more important in challenging our ideologies than Scripture. God's word contains infinite wisdom and insight into the mystery of what it means to be human (anthropology) and our capacity to discern and live out of God's grace and truth as individuals and as a community (sociology). God's Spirit uses the words of Scripture to challenge our pride and alleviate our fear. They are the most beautiful and majestic of all the forests into which we can enter, with mountains, streams, valleys, and fjords, much like Tolkien's mythical Middle-earth that has been central to Tim and Kathy's imagination and curiosity. In those seasons where we feel lost in the woods, we find in the Scriptures something like what Tolkien's character Samwise Gamgee discovered:

There, peeping among the cloud-wrack above a dark tor high up in the mountains, Sam saw a white star twinkle for a while. The beauty of it smote his heart, as he looked up out of the forsaken land, and hope returned to him. For like a shaft, clear and cold, the thought pierced him that in the end the Shadow was only a small and passing thing: there was light and high beauty forever beyond its reach.[3]

THE THIRD (AND ONLY) POINT

Anyone who has listened to a Tim Keller sermon knows that "the third point" is shorthand for the inevitable resolution of the narrative tension of his sermons: the death of Jesus on the cross. This now familiar formula was radically new to me (and I would say many who grew up in evangelical churches) and changed the way I understood the Bible and the gospel. I remember my mom, who would visit from time to time, saying once that she always felt good about being a Christian when leaving a Redeemer worship service. The subtext of that statement reveals a lot about the experience of most Christians and their understanding of what it means to follow Jesus. There are times of course when the Spirit will impress upon our hearts a weight that disturbs us into repentance, but the more obvious implication of my mom's statement is that most times the weight of moralism is thrust upon the congregant's back as they begin another week. "Do good. Be good. Or else."

Tim's consistent and relentless application of the good news of the cross to every text he preached, taught, or wrote about flows from his own conviction and relationship with God and is anything but formulaic. Our hearts are like my grandmother's old concrete birdbath. Each day in the winter she would have to go out and break the ice so that the birds could access the water. Deep insecurity lurks in the human heart, manifesting itself in a cold self-righteousness and brittle fear. I myself am a recovering Pharisee who finds it much easier to convey moralism than grace in my preaching, teaching, and living. This is why my congregation has heard me say over and over again that it is the "work of a lifetime to live as if you are loved." It's the love of God in the sacrifice of Jesus that needs to be experienced again and again, not just for our own hearts but also because it is the heart of the mission of the church. In Tim's booklet on "How to Reach the West Again" his analysis once again comes back to the "third (and only) point":

We must never lose grasp of the difference between gospel grace and religious moralism. Why does the Protestant church constantly fall into the temptation to self-righteousness, dominance, and exclusion? Why does it fail to reproduce the early church's social mandate? Because it loses its grip on the very core of its faith.[4]

The historical impact of the crazy idea of planting Redeemer Presybyterian Church in Manhattan in 1989 will be written by individuals smarter than I am. But the foolishness of the gospel of grace that was proclaimed and lived by Tim and Kathy and the community of fellow pilgrims who I've had the enormous privilege to get to know over the years has saved me from a life of looking at a place like New York City the way Jonah looked at the Ninevites. My incredulity at this "crazy idea" was the deeply rooted belief that God loved me because I was a good Baptist boy who went to Wheaton College. Over the past thirty years it has been the work of my lifetime to believe something far more amazing—that God loves me because He loves me. The proof of which are the scars of His Son.

Thank you, Tim and Kathy.

Soli Deo Gloria

ENDNOTES

1   Frederick Buechner, *Wishful Thinking: A Seeker's ABC* (New York: HarperCollins, 1993, orig. pub. 1973), 23.

2   Timothy Keller, *The Reason for God: Belief in an Age of Skepticism* (New York: Penguin, 2008), xxiii.

3   J.R.R. Tolkien, *The Return of the King* (New York: Del Ray, 1955), 211.

4   Timothy Keller, *How to Win the West Again: Six Essential Elements of a Missionary Encounter* (New York: Redeemer City to City, 2020), 51.

DANIEL **SPANJER**

City of God

AN AMERICAN OMBUDSMAN

Tim Keller has become, in Reformed circles, the pastor of the city. In one sense it seems strange to identify one person as "the" pastor of "the" city, but in twentieth- (and now twenty-first) century America, it makes sense. The nation has experienced significant cultural divisions over the last hundred years, but the tension between the cities and rural populations may be one of the most profound. Any election map since Nixon reveals the deep ideological chasm that now defines the nation.[1] Cities are no longer just places of high density population or merely dynamic economic zones which include great wealth and terrible poverty. Cities now seem to hold strongly to a narrow set of political positions, equaled in their dogmatism by rural populations who are committed to more conservative ideals. This political division has, in part, extended from religio-cultural differences[2] that have matured into a growing animosity between the nation's country and city populations.

As America's history has developed, the culture of rural America has remained tethered to moral and even philosophical views more aligned with evangelicalism. Rural Christians have come to see America's success as tied directly to Bible's moral norms and traditional Evangelical religious beliefs. Christians in urban centers, on the other hand, have tended more towards Liberalism and Progressivism. Focusing more on addressing entrenched inequities, urban Christians have pursued social reform at the expense of traditional theology and even traditional moral norms. Thus the nation's demographic dualism has resulted from religious as much as cultural differences.[3]

Christians in the cities and the country have diverged so drastically that by the end of the century each now blame the other both for the nation's crises; they even accuse one another of corrupting Christianity itself. From the perspective of rural Evangelicals, cities have become mission fields filled with natives who need to come under moral laws and recommit themselves to traditional Christian belief and practice. In the tensions that have ensued, the city populations have felt resented by rural Evangelicals who seem to blame all the social, racial, and economic problems that urban populations face on rampant immorality or Progressive politics. As a result, city populations have distanced themselves from evangelical religion because its political and cultural conservatism seems to ignore, or at worst exacerbate, the nation's social, racial, and economic crises. Against the traditionalism of rural culture, urban Christians see themselves as history's pathfinders who seek to redeem the City of Man, whereas rural Evangelicals have seen themselves as citizens of the City of God who are at war with the City of Man.

Since the 1970s, rural Evangelicals have made little headway in bridging either the cultural or religious gaps between themselves and the cities. Both sides seem to be at fault. Urban religious leaders seem to downplay biblical morals and traditional doctrine while rural religious leaders seemed to dismiss persistent social, racial, and economic problems.[4] To address this growing divide, many evangelical leaders looked to work in the cities. It was Tim Keller, however, who has taught evangelicals to work from the city. Rather than compromise orthodox, evangelical doctrines, he preached them with boldness. At the same time, he was willing to address the pernicious social problems endemic in American cities that many Evangelicals seemed to ignore. To serve the city, found himself calling urban populations to embrace evangelical orthodoxy and orthopraxy, even as he listened patiently to those who felt they had been harmed by the conservative approach of evangelical churches. Keller has, among other things, served the church as an *ombudsman* (an advocate responsible for sifting through and responding to complaints) for the City of God at a time when the cities were becoming ground zero in an American culture war.

The change America has experienced in its cultural and social history represents a substantial change in the Western tradition. Both Tim Keller's ministry in New York City and his wide influence have confirmed the scale of the historic transition that the nation has endured. A hundred and fifty years ago in America, as well as most of Europe, the cities would not have been contested spaces in religious and cultural conflicts.[5] For most of Western history, in fact, the cities have been the undisputed curators of culture. The cities provided religious leadership while claiming the responsibility to teach civic virtue to the rural populations.

From the rise of Ancient Greece in the West, the city had been the culmination of and guide for a given people's way of life. Rural areas, on the other hand, were largely illiterate and sparsely populated. Barbarians lived outside the cities while the cities remained places of refinement and education. In Europe's memory it was always the city that served as the "security of a whole civilized way of life."[6] According to historian George Botsford, "when Greeks said that life not lived in a city was semi-barbarous, they did not mean that the alternative was life on an open farm. They had in mind villages for these lacked the centralized and highly coordinated political life so essential for happy and rational existence."[7] For Rome as much as the Greeks, the country beyond the cities was divided by warring villages and plagued with lawlessness. Only in cities could notions of civic virtue be developed or the regulation of the people for the end of cooperation in service to the polis be accomplished.[8] Aristotle went even further. For him the polis, or city, was the only antidote to moral corruption. People, Aristotle argued, are political creatures who gather in cities in order to realize for the people "the good life." Life in the city was the telos of mankind, mankind in his most mature state.[9]

After the Greeks fell into war, Rome became, for many in the ancient world, the embodiment of the Greek principle. The power, sophistication, and democratic structure of the Roman Republic made it the most advanced civilization in the Western world. After Caesar, however, the great city became the capital of Emperors; it descended into decadence and abuse. More than any other event it was the rise of Christianity that revived the traditional view of the city.[10] Despite the restoration of civic order and religious morality after Constantine, Rome faced its greatest crisis as rural barbarians unleashed their uncivilized barrage on the hallowed pillars of the great city. Had the idea of the city failed? It was Augustine who put pen to paper to both salvage the traditional view of the city and the cultural importance of Christianity.

In his famous book, *The City of God,* Augustine Christianized the Western view of the city. In biblical teachings, God's law does reign not over a sparsely populated rural landscape, but over a city. For Augustine the city remained the most important arena of human fulfillment but not, as the Greeks had taught, under human leadership. The only city capable of teaching mankind to be its best is one that obeys a divine government. As Rome crumbled around him, Augustine called Christians back to the city—not to Rome, which was built around love of self, but to the kingdom of heaven, which is constructed around love of God. Thus according to Augustine, people have the choice to belong to one of two cities, each one defined by a set of core values that determine the meaning of human fulfillment. In the City of Man, the love-of-self defines its politics, its social structures, and its economics. For citizens of the City of God, on the other hand, the love-of-God directs their hearts and defines all of their interactions.[11] Augustine recognized that cities are crucially important to human life as they have the power to direct their citizens' entire lives. The question for him was not should people belong to a city, but rather should they belong to a city that cultivates in them holiness and life, or a city that sows only sin and death. His teaching deeply impacted European history throughout the Middle Ages, a time when cities became conservative forces in an otherwise wild, entropic world.

America followed European tradition during its colonial period through the early nineteenth century. Colonists imagined that their cities did more than serve as schools of virtue—their cities were bringing the heavenly city to earth for the sake of the wilderness that lay all around. Colonists understood that cities led the religious life of the New World as they established leading churches in their largest towns. John Winthrop, Boston's first governor, expressed most clearly the colonial hope for the city in his sermon "On Christian Charity," which he delivered aboard the *Arabella* in 1630 on his way to Boston.

> We shall find that the God of Israel is among us, when ten of us shall be able to resist a thousand of our enemies; when He shall make us a praise and glory that men shall say of succeeding plantations, "May the Lord make it like that of New England." For we must consider that we shall be as a city upon a hill. The eyes of all people are upon us. So that if we shall deal falsely with our God in this work we have undertaken, and so cause Him to withdraw His present help from us, we shall be made a story and a by-word through the world.[12]

Charleston, Richmond, Philadelphia, Boston, and Baltimore became culturally conservative capitals which all looked to become cities on hills which colonists constructed around institutional religion. In the New World the cities of men were the places most dedicated to the City of God.

But cities in America were becoming very different spaces at the dawn of the nineteenth century. They were increasingly important for their ports of trade or as centers of immigration rather than their cultural leadership. For many Americans, big cities became markets of economic exchange and wealth, while immigration only seemed to expand populations of impoverished people. Increasingly Christians saw the cities as mission fields rather than centers of the young nation's religious life. Christian reform movements in the antebellum period set out not to convert the wilderness but to save the city, for their leaders believed that as the cities went, so went the nation.[13] In fact, events changed the cities so quickly that in America the roles of city and country reversed. The Potato Famine of the 1840s and the rapid industrialization of the post-Civil War period altered the American city.[14] Americans who once perceived cities as conservative bastions of culture and religion came to see these same urban centers as barbarian lands of lawlessness and irreligion. Social problems, which increasingly became endemic in urban regions, were seen as the natural effects of irreligion and immorality.

David Moberg, the eminent American sociologist, notes that Evangelical Christianity made a novel decision in the 1890s. Although American Christian institutions and leaders had made addressing social ills central to their mission, they turned away from urban centers in what he called the "Great Reversal."[15] The Bible Belt came to see the city as a foreign place that shattered the harmony of Judeo-Christian values, Protestant conversion, biblical literacy, and individual industriousness. By the 1890s revivalists, reformers, and preachers went into the northern cities not as reformers bent on reclaiming their cultural and religious centers, but rather as rescue workers tasked with putting people off of so many sinking ships. For a new breed of Fundamentalists religion no longer served culture; religion became a means of converting people to make them ready for the next life, not necessarily to improve this one.

In that same period, a new group of reformers came to see the city in a new way. Progressive reformers believed that cities did not represent the tragic devolution of their classical selves, but rather laboratories which allowed specialists to engineer a new world.[16] The city no longer served the highest civic character of mankind; it was now a grand opportunity to repair the social evils that have always plagued mankind. A new breed of activists employed organization, planning, and centralization to remake American society by reforming the cities which alone could endure the economic and social changes necessary to remake human life. The Progressive movement helped inaugurate a new era in the nation's history. Traditional values were no longer the foundation for a successful civic state, rather they were so many obstacles to the kinds of change that America needed to embrace if it was to be part of the historic evolution of human culture.[17]

Many urban Christians took on the Progressive view. Between 1870 and 1890 novel Christian movements appeared in American cities: New Theol-

ogy, Protestant Liberalism, and the Social Gospel movement. These movements saw that conservative Evangelicals had ignored temporal evils while
busying themselves saving people for eternity and so came to disagree with
Augustine about the City of Man. Liberal Progressives saw that the love of
self was not humanity's chief problem but rather a potential that reformers
could leverage to make a new society free from oppression. They rejected
Augustine's dichotomy between the Cities of Man and of God because it had
only instilled an escapist mentality into traditional Christianity. But history
had now given Christians unprecedented opportunities to change the human condition. Progressives set out to change the human condition, while
Evangelicals, on the other hand, doubled down on the otherworldly commitments that had metastasized into conservative reactions to human progress.
These new theologians would transform the humanity through the city, not
try to save people out of it.

In response to the convulsive changes brought on by the end of the nineteenth century, Evangelicals also came to see the city differently. They saw
the social, economic, and racial problems of the human city as inescapable
realities of sin, not merely the result of inequities. This change was, in part,
inspired by a pessimistic eschatology known as premillennialism: a theology which emphasized the hopelessness of the City of Man. This too was a
shift in Western Christianity, as Evangelicals no longer perceived the city as
the space for civic improvement or the school of social harmony.[18] Civic and
social reform became, for the Fundamentalist movement, suspect as either a
cause entirely lost or as a subversive assault on the City of God. Keller notes
that "in the mind of many orthodox Christians, therefore, 'doing justice' is in-
extricably linked with the loss of sound doctrine and spiritual dynamism."[19]
Thus Evangelicals saw that liberal and progressive Christians sought to
leverage the love of self to make a new, more equal society.

Through the first half of the twentieth century, the cultural divide expanded and contracted as the nation faced rolling crises. World War I, the
Roaring Twenties, economic depressions (including the Great Depression),
and World War II further distanced rural from urban cultures, but dulled
the polemical spirit. Patriotism and economic hardship seemed to create shared experiences that pushed cultural tensions to the back pages of
newspapers. At moments, such as during the Scopes Monkey Trial in 1925
America seemed to be harboring a deeper divide between urban, educated
elite and rural traditionalists than people guessed. At other moments, like
the race riots occurring between 1900 and 1943, the nation was forced to

come face-to-face with unresolved animosities that threatened its very existence. Despite the gravity of these moments, Americans seemed only casually aware of cultural tension. Hidden beneath majoritarian patriotism, these wounds continued to fester until World War II ended and, with it, the unity the nation had fostered to win it. Over the subsequent forty years years, America's victory in that war would come to be seen as maybe its most divisive act. A majority of Americans, most of whom lived in the rural parts of the nation, saw World War II as proof that the nation's moral commitments, combined with Judeo-Christian beliefs, proved its moral superiority. Urban poor and minorities, however, saw America using the fight for liberty abroad as a means of covering up its own injustices at home.

The self-confidence America gained from World War II did not make sense to those suffering in urban ghettos or to progressives who were suspicious of America's conservative values. For these, America may have won a world war in support of its moral values, but that success stunted its growth and progress. According to Keller, "a 'basic shift of mood' and crisis of confidence occurred, with regard not only to older ideals of patriotism and national pride but also to traditional moral values—particularly sexual mores. The very idea of moral authority began to be questioned."[20]

Several fault lines appeared in the nation's cultural landscape in the postwar period.[21] Older and rural populations solidified their commitment to values in line with evangelical and traditional lifestyles. For example, Billy Graham's success came from a simple gospel message—human suffering and social problems would be solved by conversion, followed by a commitment to moral living.[22] For younger people and urban populations, however, "the gospel message was not simply being rejected; it was becoming incomprehensible and increasingly hated. The world that Christians in the West had known—where the culture tilted in the direction of traditional Christianity—no longer existed. The culture had become a problem the church could no longer ignore."[23] The cultural skirmishes that broke out in the 1890s had become a full-scale war. As the Cold War developed, it seemed that any common ground between the two sides was evaporating at an unprecedented rate.

As the end of the twentieth century came into view, American Christians faced the ugly reality that they were as divided as their culture. "By the mid-1990s there was a growing sense that the conservative churches of the US were fast losing contact with culture and society, despite the fact that in the late 1970s and early '80s the seeker-church movement had sought to make the church more appealing to contemporary people."[24] The City of God now represented an out-of-touch religious tradition that no longer made sense to the cities of men. Its values appeared dated, or worse, irrelevant to the urban problems of a postmodern world.[25] At the same time, urban leaders and even churches lost touch with the historic doctrines that had informed the Christian faith since Paul.

The struggles of the American church are not new to the history of redemption. Since God's people are also sinners, it is not surprising to find bigotry, violence, and division in the story of His church. However, in His great love for the church, He has never left it to wander off into the darkness. According to His own timing He raises up voices who call the church back to Him. Of course God does not need people to defend His ways, but it appears that He employs ombudsmen who must patiently hear from those who have suffered from His church's failures and share with them God's character, love, and salvation.

It could be that for this time in history and in this place, God called Tim Keller to serve as an ombudsman for His kingdom. Tim Keller came through seminary during the convulsions of culture war in the 1960s. Like most evangelical leaders, he knew that something was seriously wrong in the American church. Urban and Progressive leaders saw the nation's social, racial, and economic crises clearly but evidenced no commitment to the historic truths of Christianity. Rural and conservative leaders remained steadfastly committed to the historic truths of Christianity but were seemingly unconcerned about the deep social problems faced mostly by urban and minority communities.

One of the insights that Keller has made for the sake of the American church is that traditional Christian morals and doctrines entail a vision of justice. In other words, one of the key errors which may have contributed to the brokenness of American Christianity is a dangerous reductionism. More conservative, rural Evangelicals have faithfully taught right morals and doctrines to the exclusion of the political implications of those morals and doctrines. By political implications, Keller means that right belief about God assumes that He is the King. In other words, the gospel cannot not be political. Calling people to embrace Christ's death and resurrection necessarily entails calling Him king. "The most traditional formulation of evangelical doctrine, rightly understood," Keller claims, "should lead its proponents to a life of doing justice in the world."[26]

In addition to restoring a political dimension to evangelical thought, Keller has also patiently listened to the complaints of those who have struggled in a predominantly Christian culture. Ministering in Manhattan, Keller witnessed not only the deep social evils of urban life, but also heard the pain of those who felt forgotten by the church. To this pain Keller has spoken clearly: "God loves and defends those with the least economic and social power, and so should we. That is what it means to 'do justice.'"[27] The City of God is not only a place out of this world for those who are saved by Christ's sacrifice, it is also the source of justice for this broken world. While American Christians may have courageously preached the gospel of redemption, they have, at times, forgotten to speak of God's love for those who suffer in this life. "(God's) goal for the poor is a life of delight, and his goal for the widow is that her eye would 'no longer be weary.' He is not at all satisfied with halfway measures for the needy people in his community. He is not content to give them small perfunctory gifts in the assumption that their misery and weakness are a permanent condition."[28]

While Keller has clearly understood the pain of those around him, he has also represented his King to the city. For Keller there is ultimately no justice or goodness where the gospel of the King's death and resurrection is not spoken. Keller has warned those who seek justice in the city that without the gospel human efforts to realize justice in society actually point people away from their true and ultimate problem, which is not social inequity but sin. When people do not recognize that rebellion against God is the actual source of all suffering, they attempt to replace Christ with their own versions of a king. "When we decide to be our own center, our own king, everything falls apart: physically, socially, spiritually, and psychologically."[29] Without God, human efforts to realize justice are ultimately futile because they cannot finally give people their true identity which only comes from God through faith in the completed work of Christ. This is the heart, lungs, and blood of the Gospel, which is the starting point not only for all Christian belief, but for all Christian social action as well.

Keller has been clear that any alteration of the Gospel not only distances the believer from his God but fatally corrupts any effort to solve social evils. It could be that both conservative Evangelicals and liberal Protestants have, at times, forgotten this. The ombudsman of the kingdom, the herald of Christ the king, must cry out that salvation only comes through the atoning work of Christ. "'This is what has been done in history. This is how Jesus lived and died to earn the way to God for you.' Christianity is completely different (than religious advice about what you have to do to connect to God). It's joyful news."[30]

Together the political character of Christ's kingship and the gospel message must, Keller argues, become the core that restores harmony to His church. Only when the Church preaches the political character of Christ's kingship and proclaims that people can only seek Him only through the gospel can it put back together what is broken. Keller has helped explain that the church is divided because Christians have allowed truth and love to be pulled apart. It has been common practice for conservative Evangelicals not only to identify the errors in those who abandoned traditional Christian belief and behavior, but then to accuse them for the failures of the modern church. Liberal Progressive Christians have taken the inverse of the same position. These claim that conservative Evangelicals have weakened the church by not taking social concerns seriously enough. The former build their churches on the cornerstone of truth but forget love, while the latter build on love but devalue truth. Keller calls Christians to build the church on Christ who is the only foundation, the King who is both truth and love.

The only solution for American churches is to reunite truth and love under the reign of King Jesus. Pursuing truth without love has made some Christians reactionary and combative. In a noble effort to protect the historic traditions of Christianity, conservative Evangelicals have, at times, championed truth at the expense of compassion. On the other hand, love that is not anchored in truth amounts to little more than the desire to make people happy without pointing them to Christ who is their only hope. Progressive Christians often exhibit great compassion for their neighbors but do not clearly call people to obey Christ. For Keller, the City of God offers the American church the only model of wholeness able to restore its glory. For the heavenly city is the place where the King reigns in truth and love. As Christ cannot be broken into these two things, so His church cannot stand unless under Christ it embraces both.

Thus Keller seeks to restore Augustine's commitment to the city as a place of tension between great human potential and grievous evil.[31] The city is a place where many humans work and live under their Creator, who is not a distant savior but a living and reigning king. His love is not abstract; it is political. His laws are not merely moral but social. King Jesus will save His people from their sins as He rescues them into His kingdom. The truth is that "A true king will come back to put everything right and renew the entire world. The good news of the kingdom of God is this: Jesus is that true King."[32] As king, Christ is the one person in whom truth and love are fully realized, so the church must hold both of these simultaneously and courageously.

"We should not think of Christians out in the world as merely distinct and detached individuals. They are still the body of Christ, the Church. As Christians in this world, they are still to think and work together, banding together in creative forms, being the Church organic that the Church institutional has discipled them to be."[33]

Participation in the City of God does not require Christians to leave the City of Man, but rather to be His representatives to all people. Thus Christians should commit themselves to human cities as witnesses to the resurrected Lord. This will do two things for them. First, it will free the Christian to serve his king anywhere and everywhere. Second, it will bind the Christian to serving his king anywhere and everywhere. Religions other than Christianity "all have the same logic: If I perform, if I obey, I'm accepted." But human effort alone cannot restore to human beings that which they need the most. "The gospel of Jesus," argues Keller, "is not only different from that but diametrically opposed to [gospels of human effort]: I'm fully accepted in Jesus Christ, and therefore I obey."[34]

> But in the life of Christians the law of God—though still binding on them—functions in a completely different way. It shows you the life of love you want to live before the God who has done so much for you. God's law takes you out of yourself; it shows you how to serve God and others instead of being absorbed with yourself. You study and obey the law of God in order to discover the kind of life you should live in order to please and resemble the one who created and redeemed you, delivering you from the consequences of sin.[35]

Keller has ministered in the city from the overlapping areas of a historically Christian Venn diagram—where the historic doctrines of Christianity meet the pursuit of justice in this broken world. He makes this clear in what may be his most enduring work, *The Prodigal God*. In Keller's assessment, the older son remained upright and committed to traditional biblical morals. But the older son became twisted by his own righteousness. He may have believed that his father was a good and upright man and even paid his father the proper respect. However, his righteousness proved to be more self-serving than it appeared, and his respect hid a dangerous jealousy that fatally weakened his character. What looked to everyone around him like loving service to his father devolved into a selfishness which hardened his heart. Jesus' listeners might rightly have asked, how could the older son love his father and not be reformed by the tender forgiveness the father showed to his repentant younger son?

Neither was the younger son the model of uprightness. It would be easy in our postmodern culture to lionize the younger son for finding his own way while mocking the traditions that held him back. But the decision to "be himself" was not without terrible cost. The younger son's decision to follow his own heart ruined his father's reputation and nearly destroyed the family to which he owed respect and honor. The decision seemed exciting at first. He cut himself from the moral constraints of his father's authority so that he could live out his own passions. But the older son could have predicted what harvest that decision would yield. Social and economic disorder plagued the younger son who abandoned traditional values to embark on a lascivious way of life.

In these two brothers Tim Keller saw the dysfunction that has come to define the American church. Like the older son, traditional churches "held to the traditional morality of their upbringing,"[36] and so have remained faithful to orthodox beliefs and morals. Rather than move into the cosmopolitan cities to find their own way, conservatives "[grew] up, [took] conventional job(s), and [settled] down near mom and dad."[37] But their uprightness keeps them from seeing "their blindness, narrowness, and self-righteousness, and how these things are destroying both their own souls and the lives of people around them."[38] Could it be that the lack of responsiveness among evangelical churches to the nation's social, economic, and racial evils reveals hearts that, like that of the older brother, have been hardened?

On the other hand, the liberal Progressives have left "the traditional morality of their families and respectable society,"[39] "to live in the hip-shabby neighborhoods of New York and Los Angeles."[40] The progressive and liberal churches have concluded that orthodox belief and morals are oppressive constraints. To solve the inequities in their communities, they have asked for their cultural and religious inheritance, which they spent without reference to the traditions of their faith. Could it be that these Christians needed to hear the call to return in repentance? Rather than justify themselves by judging conservative Evangelicals, they should seek true freedom in obedience to the church's historic teachings.

Keller summarizes his discussion of the two brothers in a way that allows it to be a pattern for more than just Samaritans and Pharisees. "The hearts of the two brothers were the same. Both sons resented their father's authority and sought ways of getting out from under it. They each wanted to get into a position in which they could tell the father what to do. Each one, in other words, rebelled—but one did so by being very bad and the other by being extremely good. Both were alienated from their father's heart; both were lost sons."[41] From his pulpit, lectern, and pen the ombudsman has called out to the hurting city and the divided church: come back to King Jesus in whom is salvation from sin—to Christ, who is the only way back to the good, just, and perfect Father.

ENDNOTES

1   See Dante J. Scala and Kenneth M. Johnson, "Political Polarization Along the Rural-Urban Continuum? The Geography of the Presidential Vote, 2000–2016," *The ANNALS of the American Academy of Political and Social Science* 672, no. 1 (2017).

2   For more on the relationship between religion and culture in America's internal divisions, see James Davidson Hunter, *Culture Wars: The Struggle to Define America* (New York: Basic Books, 1991), and James L. Nolan, *The American Culture Wars: Current Contests and Future Prospects* (Charlottesville: University Press of Virginia, 1996).

3   Although Chalfant published his article over thirty years ago, it presents research from the previous twenty years which strongly supports the fact that urban and rural residencies have a serious impact on the degree to which a religious person's views are traditional (rural) or non-traditional (urban). H. Paul Chalfant and Peter L. Heller, "Rural/Urban Versus Regional Differences in Religiosity," *Review of Religious Research* 33, no. 1 (1991).

4   Timothy Keller, *The Prodigal God: Recovering the Heart of the Christian Faith* (New York: Dutton, 2008), 12–13.

5   Beginning with the work of J.G.A. Pocock, historians have become aware of the tension between the country and the cities in England during the seventeenth and eighteenth centuries. John Greville Agard Pocock, *The Machiavellian Moment: Florentine Political Thought and the Atlantic Republican Tradition* (Princeton, N.J.: Princeton University Press, 1975).

6   Peter Brown, *Augustine of Hippo: A Biography* (Berkley: University of California Press, 2013)., 287.

7   George Willis Botsford, Charles Alexander Robinson, and Donald Kagan, *Botsford and Robinson's Hellenic History* ([New York: Macmillan, 1970), 52.

8   Keller notes that in the Bible, the city was the place of civilization: "Cities were places where life was not dangerously out of control." Timothy Keller, *Loving the City: Doing Balanced, Gospel-Centered Ministry in Your City* (Grand Rapids, MI: Zondervan, 2016), 115.

9   Aristotle and Richard McKeon, *The Basic Works of Aristotle* (New York: Modern Library, 2001), 1129.

10   Keller, *Loving the City*, 132.

11   Augustine, *The City of God* (New York: Modern Library, 2000), 477ff

12   John Winthrop, *The Journal of John Winthrop, 1630–1649*, ed. Richard S. Dunn and Laetitia Yeandle (Cambridge, MA: Harvard University Press, 1996).

13   See, Ronald G. Walters, *American Reformers, 1815–1860* (New York: Hill and Wang, 1978).

14   For an interesting study of how the urban/rural divide, among other factors, impacted the way that churches responded to issues such as race, see Lucas P. Volkman, *Houses Divided: Evangelical Schisms and the Crisis of the Union in Missouri* (New York: Oxford University Press, 2018).

15   David Moberg, *Great Reversal: Reconciling Evangelism and Social Concern* ((Eugene, OR: Wipf & Stock Publishers, 2007). See also George Marsden's excellent discussion of this phenomenon: George M. Marsden, *Fundamentalism and American Culture: The Shaping of Twentieth Century Evangelicalism, 1870–1925* (New York: Oxford University Press, 1980)., 85ff.

16 See, Robert H. Wiebe and David Donald, *The Search for Order: 1877–1920*. (New York: Hill and Wang, 1967); James T. Kloppenberg, "The Virtues of Liberalism: Christianity, Republicanism, and Ethics in Early American Political Discourse," *The Journal of American History* 74, no. 1 (1987).

17 John Patrick Diggins, *The Promise of Pragmatism: Modernism and the Crisis of Knowledge and Authority* (Chicago: University of Chicago, 1994).

18 Keller, *Loving the City*, 113.

19 Timothy Keller, *Generous Justice: How God's Grace Makes Us Just* (New York: Riverhead Books, 2010), xvi.

20 Keller, *Loving the City*, 196.

21 Keller, *Prodigal God*, 12.

22 Consider this summary from Billy Graham's book, *Peace with God*: "Christ came to give us the answers to the three enduring problems of sin, sorrow, and death. It is Jesus Christ, and He alone, who is also enduring and unchanging, 'the same yesterday, and today and forever.'" Billy Graham, *Peace with God: The Secret of Happiness* (Nashville, TN: Thomas Nelson, 2011), 7.

23 Keller, *Loving the City*, 197.

24 Keller, *Loving the City*, 199.

25 Sarah Pulliam Bailey made an interesting argument after the 2016 election when she argued that the race to do missions in the cities distracted evangelicals from the social ills faced by rural communities. Sarah Pulliam Bailey, "Some Evangelicals Question Whether They Have Overlooked the Rural Church," *Washington Post*, December 15, 2016, https://www.washingtonpost.com/news/acts-of-faith/wp/2016/12/15/some-evangelicals-question-whether-they-have-overlooked-the-rural-church/

26 Keller, *Generous Justice*, xiii.

27 Keller, *Generous Justice*, 5.

28 Keller, *Generous Justice*, 14.

29 Timothy Keller, *Jesus the King: Understanding the Life and Death of the Son of God* (New York: Penguin Books, 2011), 17.

30 Keller, *Loving the City*, 16.

31 Keller, *Loving the City*, 113ff.

32 Keller, *Jesus the King*, 18.

33 Keller, *Loving the City*, 267.

34 Keller, *Jesus the King*, 42.

35 Keller, *Jesus the King*, 43–44.

36 Keller, *Prodigal God*, 8.

37 Keller, *Prodigal God*, 11.

38 Keller, *Prodigal God*, 10.

39 Keller, *Prodigal God*, 8.

40 Keller, *Prodigal God*, 11.

41 Keller, *Prodigal God*, 36.

A.D. **BAUER**

Prayer

PREPARING THE CITY FOR CHRIST'S RETURN

If we think about the content of our prayers, certain themes seem to repeat. Most of us pray for our families, friends, and neighbors; we will say a special word for those who are sick. We often talk to God about events in our lives today or about things that are coming up. But we rarely consider the big picture: the church of Jesus Christ that extends beyond our own local congregations, the pastors we know and support, the men and women serving the Lord in difficult places around the globe, or the leadership of our denominations. For the purpose of this article, I would like to draw our attention to our need to pray for our cities.

When I lived in the suburbs, I lived a comfortable Christian lifestyle in what might be called the suburban Christian ghetto. Most of the challenges I heard from preachers had to do with personal growth and holiness. But even those challenges were comfortable because they did not take me outside of my snug, comfy existence. Is that a concern? I believe so.

God is attentive to the circumstances of all people, but He expresses a particular concern for certain groups. Jesus' words and actions toward children show us He has a special love for them. God is also interested in the welfare of cities. Jonah was sent to a city where 120,000 people are described as not knowing their right hand from their left. God sent Jonah to prevent their destruction. Jesus speaks of His love for Jerusalem and His desire to protect them. Dr. Keller also observes that "In Genesis we see every one of the patriarchs—Abraham, Isaac, and Jacob—praying with familiarity and directness. Abraham's doggedly insistent prayer for God's mercy on the pagan cities of Sodom and Gomorrah is remarkable (Gen. 18:23ff)."[1] It makes sense that God would have exceptional affection for places where His image bearers gather. If God has a special love for cities, we should as well.

I believe God calls for many of us to pray for cities and particularly for the city closest to our home. Those living outside the city might find it helpful to think about what praying for that city involves. As Dr. Keller observes in his book *Prayer*, "Lifting up our desires with a view to God's wisdom has one more effect on our petitions that we have not mentioned. We must ask ourselves 'what we ourselves might need to do to implement answers to our prayers.' To some degree the answers to many of our petitions would be facilitated by changes in *us*, but we usually do not take time to consider this as we pray."[2]

Considering the role we may be called to play in contributing to the answering of our prayers is one way we carry our cross. It appears that the comfort I experienced in my earlier years is the opposite of the sacrifice to which we are called. When I look at Scripture, I don't see Jesus or the disciples making themselves comfortable. Other than a brief period right after the crucifixion, the disciples are not huddling together in their safe space. Rather, they are out there, proclaiming a message that is unpopular among the political and religious elites. The temptation I experienced was to surround myself with Christian friends in my local church and neighborhood and live in an environment where I avoided scary situations. God calls us to move beyond that kind of comfort, to face the unexpected and unknown, so we can spread the gospel.

The city can be a frightening place for many suburban and rural Christians. Most of us live close enough to a city that we consider it to be our own. We might root for the metropolitan sport teams or tell people we are from that city. For most of my life my city has been Baltimore. While I considered myself as being from Baltimore, as a suburbanite, I did not really care about the city. I believed in the importance of prayer but until my pastor called for his congregation to pray for Baltimore, I don't think I had prayed for my city one time.

There are lots of reasons we might not pray for our city. When I lived in the suburbs Baltimore was "over there." I could visit the city for sports, concerts, or museums, but I did not live in the city. I would not go into the city without a specific purpose because Baltimore is a dangerous place. I didn't know many people who actually lived in Baltimore, so it was hard to really care about the city. From my perspective, the city was filled with political corruption, poverty, gangs, and garbage in the streets. Somehow that did not draw me to pray for revival of the church in the city.

All of that may be why the Lord took a man who lived in the suburbs and moved him to the city. I have now lived in Baltimore city with my family for more than thirty years. For some that might seem like a scary proposition. Baltimore has a reputation for being a violent city and the murder rate is very high. On more than one occasion, while I was traveling in Europe, people would ask where I was from. Often their knowledge of American geography was limited to New York and Washington, DC. But when I said I was from Baltimore, many recognized the city and made reference to the television show *The Wire*. I suppose that is what Baltimore is best known for in some circles.

While I spent most of my life in the suburbs, my wife grew up in the city and, until she married me, attended the same city church. We lived outside Philadelphia for a while, and when we returned to Baltimore, we moved into the city neighborhood where my wife had grown up. This was the initial impetus for us to live in the city. We have never left.

Our current house is on a fairly quiet street and we have a number of good neighbors. We have experienced some of the less desirable features of city life. We've had our home broken into and had cars and other items stolen; we've heard loud voices late at night, and we do hear the occasional gunshots. But we enjoy having so many places in walking distance: stores, libraries, churches, and the like. It is a short drive to wooded hiking trails, wonderful museums, and many styles of restaurants.

After we moved within the city, for a variety of reasons, we were looking for a new church to attend. My daughter suggested we try a church plant that was five minutes away from our house. We had heard of Dr. Keller and his work in planting churches in New York. The idea of helping plant a church in our city seemed attractive. Our focus then and now has been the centrality of the gospel preached from the word of God in context. This church had a reputation for biblical preaching. But of course, you never know what a church is going to be like until you attend it.

The church was meeting in a school. Years earlier I had pastored a church plant in suburban Philadelphia that met in a school; I had also been an interim pastor for a church outside Baltimore that met in a school. The building atmosphere in a gym or cafeteria does not present a view that reminds one of the glory of God. If you have been to a European cathedral, the tall ceilings and surrounding beauty are almost the opposite of a school gym. In the absence of beauty, it takes a great church community and excellent preaching to draw your attention toward God.

I was not excited about worshipping in a gym, and I was not so sure I wanted to attend a Baptist church. I had attended a Baptist church when I was five, but for many decades after that I was in Presbyterian or Episcopal churches. I was ordained in a Presbyterian church. I transferred to an Episcopal denomination when I was called to be pastor of an Episcopal church. I had wrestled with the issue of believer's baptism and had come down firmly on the side of baptizing infants. I even had a mostly completed manuscript for a book explaining how Scripture supported infant baptism.

However, none of these concerns were disqualifying, because what my wife and I wanted most of all in a church was good preaching in a community of believers who cared for each other. What we were looking for was a church home where we could fit in and belong.

As we entered the gym, my first impression was that I was one of the oldest people in the church. It was also surprising that the church was the most racially diverse congregation I had ever seen or heard of. Though Baltimore city is majority black with a significant number of whites, Hispanics, and Asians, its churches tend to be monochrome. There are white churches, black churches, Hispanic churches, and Asian churches. Even churches that resist being monochrome tend to have one race dominate in the congregation. Most of the city churches I had attended were like suburban churches. In many cases, the churches retained their same look and feel as the neighborhood around them changed. As people left the local community and moved to the suburbs, those families would often continue to drive into the city to attend what they considered to be their church. In contrast, this church plant was a good picture of the East Baltimore area where we lived. It looked like our neighborhood.

During our first few weeks at this new church plant, our hope was to hear the word of God presented in a compelling way. As we listened to the sermons, we were struck by how clearly the pastor preached the gospel. He taught what was in the biblical text and did an excellent job of showing how that text should be lived out. In many ways this reminded us of Tim Keller's preaching, which we had heard through recordings and once in person. This was the beginning of a new adventure: learning how to fit into a church that was completely outside the norms of our culture and experience.

It was clear that participating in this church would be different than other churches where we had worshipped, and questions came to mind as we continued attending services. Were believers of different races able to share a common vision and coexist in harmony? What would we experience attending a place where almost every member was significantly younger than we were? Would we fit in?

The differences compared with our previous church attendance challenged us to rethink our role. It did not take long for us to determine that this local church plant was where we needed to worship. We love liturgical worship, and good theology is critical to our participation in any church. We knew we were giving up our liturgical services, but this new church had good theology and teaching that exceeded our initial expectations. So we found ourselves in a Baptist church where so many elements were a brand-new experience to us. The culture shock was real, but there was one overriding element that we could not ignore: this was a church where we heard the gospel proclaimed with greater clarity than we had found elsewhere.

The importance of excellent biblical preaching cannot be overstated. My wife, who is a biblical counselor, has observed that relationship and behavioral issues in peoples' lives are more easily addressed by a counselor when those people sit under good preaching. It also appeared to us that the excellent preaching reduced conflict, creating a greater sense of unity in the church as most people worked out how to live the gospel. The opportunity God provided for us to move into a very different church environment was a challenge filled with blessings. We made many valued friends, learned more about ourselves, and experienced increased growth as we were called to give more of ourselves to serve God in this new setting.

By bringing me to a diverse city church, God confronted my tendency to choose what is comfortable rather than picking up my cross. It is natural for all of us to remain in what is comfortable rather than facing the uncertain and the unknown. We have all seen believers who have been called to give up their comforts to spread the gospel. Throughout history the universal church has progressed as believers have travelled with the gospel. Sometimes people have left their homes and gone to faraway lands. Sometimes the trip is shorter but the change in culture can be just as unsettling. Whether they go to communities that have not heard God's word or they proclaim the gospel to people with a nominal faith, the process of being uprooted to go elsewhere is difficult but rewarding.

I would hope that many of our church experiences are joyful, fulfilling, and satisfying. I know that for me there is always a danger that my church experience could become an end in itself. In the past, I became comfortable in a way that tended to distract me from my devotion to Christ. I imagine that for many of us there is a sort of ordinariness, a routine, that is common in our experience of church. We do the same things, in the same order, at the same time, in the same way, over and over again. That comfortable repetition can feel nice, but is it what we are called to do as salt and light in the world?

Sometimes God leads us in a certain direction and we don't realize where He is taking us until we get there. Some of you may be more situationally aware so that God's leading is less surprising to you than it has been for me. For my family, God unexpectedly brought us into an environment unlike anything we had ever experienced. I was constantly surprised by what I found.

For example, I don't like rap music. But in this church, I heard talented men doing rap and spoken word that captured my heart. Imagine hearing excellent theology and the gospel message sung and said in a form that drew you toward greater love for God. These young men had a faith and a message that spoke to and instructed me. I had to change all my preconceived notions about music and performances.

The people I met were totally different than anyone else I knew. For many of them, their experiences growing up in Baltimore city reflected the destructive cultural norms so prevalent in the city. Some had grown up without their fathers and had lived under the constant threat of violence or poverty. Yet, like me, they had struggles in their everyday lives. Some had big dreams, and they may accomplish their goals one day. Others desired to build a family devoted to God. Some were scholars—they knew more about books than I ever will.

People used their gifts to share the work and the joy of ministry—there was a high level of participation within the church. Most of us helped take down chairs. Some came early to do the setup. People helped with the nursery. In these shared responsibilities there was a bond of caring for each other. There was an openness about peoples' struggles that I had never seen in my suburban churches. By knowing what was going on in one another's lives we were all able to pray more specifically for each other. Additionally, there was little, if any, gossip. That gave people the freedom to be more honest about who they were.

I was reminded recently of how my experience in the church has changed through God's taking my life in a different direction. For many years I had not had the chance to participate in a men's group. Now I find myself in two different groups. One group is sponsored by my local church. It is wonderful to get to know some of the men during our monthly meetings. The second group is an online gathering of believers, men from different cities and different churches, where we talk about what is going on in our lives. What is unique about this second group is that I was invited to join this group by a rap artist who at one time attended our church. As a result, I find myself sharing my experiences with a group of predominantly young Black men who use this forum to encourage each other in the Lord. I find myself blessed by the openness, wisdom, and commitment to serve Jesus found in this group. I am, in many ways, culturally and racially an outsider, but through Jesus I am welcomed and made part of this group.

You might be saying to yourself, that is all fine for you but what is your point? Are you saying the people living in the suburbs should uproot themselves and attend a city church? Are we all supposed to do what you are doing?

That is not at all what I am saying. My move to the city was not an intentional repudiation of comfort and the suburban lifestyle. What happened in my life was the result of God directing circumstances so that I moved to the city. Then, progressively, He led me to a particular church. By bringing me to that church, God worked to change me. One important thing God taught me was how poorly I prayed. It was encouraging to read Dr. Keller's statement that prayer is very hard. I needed to be more devoted to prayer and conscious of the needs of our church, and our city. Dr, Keller observes that, "Prayer is not merely a way to get inward peace—it is also a way to look outward and participate with God in his work in the world."[3] This is why our city church has embraced the statement "Prayer is our Primary Strategy." This has been my path, and attending a new church in the city has been energizing for me and my family. However, this is not the path everyone is called to take.

In contrast, what I am saying is that we may need to pray for our city, and that God may require more of us than simple prayer. There will always be a level of discomfort if we are faithfully following the gospel. As each of us pick up our cross and follow Jesus, we find that the impact of the fall is constantly present. Confronting our own sins is difficult. Then we also have to interact with people (image bearers) who often are so different from us. We may have to respond appropriately to the sins of others. On top of that, life is so full of activities and the demands of family, work, and church that we are easily distracted from thinking about God's work in the world outside our immediate sphere of interest. Yet God is leading us all in some direction for the furtherance of His kingdom. For some it may involve prayer for the city and participating in God's work in the city. But for others there may be a different focus.

The city is not the only place where people sacrifice for the gospel. Rural churches have their own challenges. Pastors can feel isolated in lower population areas. There can be a real culture shock in joining a rural community where the pastor is an outsider among people who have known each other for decades. Perhaps we are called to pray for those pastors and their congregations. Or we may be led toward some other ministry focus.

Whatever direction God is taking us, we can be sure that He is in the middle of what is going on in our lives. His goal is not our comfort. But, you may ask, why is it so important for believers to face discomfort in their church lives? Shouldn't the church be a safe haven in a world that can be filled with pain, danger, and fear?

The church should be a source of comfort when we face difficulties in our lives. We need each other when we are confronted with the death of a loved one, broken relationships and physical hurts. However, this work of the church in comforting believers is only one side of our church experience.

Our bodies need rest. However, if we constantly rest, we will not develop flexibility, balance, and strength. In our religious lives we fight not against age and gravity but against the loss of the spiritual vigor to contest the Fall. Many believers embrace an alternate approach. Rather than fighting the Fall, they focus on avoiding feeling the impact of the Fall in their lives. To choose this comfort is to accept spiritual weakness and poverty.

I believe one of the reasons I never prayed for the city was that I was too comfortable. To pray for the city would require me to think about the struggle people face who live in the city. In Jesus' day he saw people in the city of Jerusalem as sheep without a shepherd. The same could be said of so many in our cities. These dear people, who bear the image of God, may not have the chance to hear the gospel with any clarity. They may hear a gospel from charlatans who enrich themselves by offering prosperity or health they have no ability to provide. Some have given up on a church they view as having nothing to offer.

I needed to learn the importance of praying and particularly how important it is for me to pray for my city. It was folly for me not to pray for the men who go into the most drug-infested and violent areas of Baltimore to offer hope and the gospel to those without hope. It was foolish that I failed to pray for the families doing all they could to raise children who know and love Jesus. How often did I miss the opportunity to pray for the city pastors who proclaim the gospel in their lives as well as in their pulpits?

There is a temptation to settle comfortably into a local church. I was always active in my church but I was also comfortable. I fear that too many of us find our lives and our church experience quite comfortable. Yet there seem to be striking similarities between a comfortable church and the church in Laodicea in Revelation. To state it directly, a comfortable believer in a comfortable church is almost certainly not prepared for the return of Christ.

One of the foundational doctrines of the church is the return of Christ. People talk about how wonderful it would be for Jesus to come again. Yet eschatological passages in the gospels give an impression that Jesus did not think most believers would be prepared for His return. There is almost a pessimism in how He talks about the end of the world. Jesus asks if when He returns, He will find faith on the earth (Luke 18:8). He also talks about the love of most (which in context means most believers) growing cold because of the increase in lawlessness (Matt. 24:10–14).

These kinds of statements warn us against succumbing to an idol of comfort. There is no comfortable way to pick up our cross each day. So, what uncomfortable thing is God calling us to do? Perhaps we should be praying for our city. Prayer may clarify where we should be participating in God's work. Perhaps we should be praying for the rural communities as well. Whatever it is God has for us to do, faithfully pursuing it will likely make us uncomfortable. But it will also prepare us and His church for His return. Therefore, when we pray, let us also pray for our cities.

ENDNOTES

1   Timothy Keller, *Prayer: Experiencing Awe and Intimacy with God* (New York: Penguin, 2014), 26.
2   Keller, *Prayer,* 229.
3   Keller, 223.

WILLIAM **EDGAR**

Hope

CAN EUROPE REALLY CHANGE?

The whole world is going to be redeemed. Jesus is going to redeem spirit and body, reason and emotion, people and nature. There is no part of reality for which there is no hope.
—Timothy Keller, *Every Good Endeavor*

Around the time of the many revolutions in 1989 and just beyond, our family used to meet for a conference in Sopron, Hungary. Right outside was a lone bunker where only a few years before defectors from communism would hide on their way to freedom in Vienna. Soon, scores—then hundreds—of refugees crossed over to safety. On August 19, 1989, there was a large peaceful demonstration right on that spot, and the road from Sopron to Austria was open for a few hours. It became known as the "Pan-European Picnic." This was one of the stepping stones, known as a *dress rehearsal*, to what would become a great stream of immigrants East to West and to freedom.

The fall of communism in many parts of the world caught even the most optimistic pundits by surprise. 1989! It was the *annus mirabilis* which saw the loosening of many satellite countries from the yoke of oppressive Russian rule. Things went fast. The images of the Berlin Wall in pieces, with celebrants drinking champagne and dancing on it, stood in stark contrast to the stories of the risky, danger-fraught escape artists of just months before. Vaclav Havel, one of the great characters from this time, went from being a jailed victim of communist control to president of Czechoslovakia. The once-illegal Solidarnosc Christian labor union led by Lech Walesa went from its underground existence to winning every seat in the Polish National Assembly.

Imre Nagy, leader of the Hungarian uprising of 1956 was exhumed and given a hero's funeral in Budapest. The tyrant Nicolae Ceaucescu was executed. The sinister forces of communism which had ruled over forty countries and produced some one hundred million victims collapsed, without any resistance. Over 1,300 monuments to Vladimir Lenin were toppled in the Ukraine alone.

Historians such as Padraic Kenney have argued that the fall of the Iron Curtain was not primarily caused by pressure from America nor from Perestroika, but because of "broad social unrest on dozens of stages."[1] I remember reading Vaclav Havel's letters to his wife from prison, where he suggested that communism was gray. If only one greengrocer could put an anti-Marxist slogan in his window, color could be restored and real change might happen (his moving *Letters to Olga* reveal himself to be a deeply flawed hero, but one who had the courage to look communism in the face and declare the emperor to be without clothes).[2]

The unusual neo-conservative economist Francis Fukuyama boldly declared that this was the end of history.[3] He did not mean there would be no more historical events, but that the goal of history, achieving democratic liberalism, had been achieved, and there seemed to be no looking back. Here is Hegel with a twist: the end of history ("The Last Man") would not be arriving at some kind of *weltgeist* but at the goal for humanity: liberal capitalism!

Historian Odd Arne Westad chronicles the Cold War in great detail. After 629 pages, he concludes that the Cold War ended in 1989 and saw the victory of capitalism over socialism.[4] In fairness, he nuances this conclusion by admitting "although the Cold War between capitalism and socialism influenced most things in the twentieth century, it did not decide everything." But it did influence most things, he goes on to say, "because of the centrality of its ideologies and the intensity of its adherents."[5]

I was in midlife during these upheavals. My greatest memory is of joy! We were all amazed and gratified at the victory of the West over the forces of communism. It was a time to celebrate.

Now, more than thirty years hence, what has happened to the new world order? The joy is gone. Scarcely anyone celebrated any of the anniversaries of the most remarkable upheaval of the twentieth century. Even the tenth anniversary was a muted affair. Only a few scattered holidays in commemoration of the events of 1989 can still be found. Germany marks November 9th, and the Czechs celebrate November 17th. But nothing in Poland, nor Hungary. Ten years after the collapse, editorials seemed more concerned with what had not changed than with what had. David Fromkin wrote that "our enemies gave up their own faith without necessarily acquiring ours," and pointed to the electoral successes of various former communists.[6] E.J. Dionne, Jr., bleakly declared that politics had "lost its epic quality"—"the world of black and white, evil empires and honorable democracies" had been replaced with "the world as it usually is, a complicated place colored more in pastels and grays."[7] This sad state of affairs looks like a return to Havel's gray society under communism, except it is not totalitarian. Fukuyama's triumphalism seemed way out of place. This was even more true of the twentieth and now the thirtieth anniversaries. I have traveled extensively in Central and Eastern Europe and have found people to be generally cheerless. To be sure, no one really wants to return to communism, yet a kind of cynicism has often replaced any sense of jubilation.

Why? A number of explanations suggest themselves. First of all, the revolutions of 1989 were not quite comprehensive. Two negative bookends put into question the undoubted achievements of 1989. The first is, of course, the tragedy of Tiananmen Square. Millions of pro-democracy Chinese citizens demonstrated, and were crushed. The protests were originally critical of party politics; they were not, as the government alleged, appeals for democracy. But in the days that followed, the army fired warning shots, then deadly assaults on the crowd, killing hundreds of protesters. In the end, the uprising was suppressed. One of my Chinese friends, who had believed in the possibility of progress, was completely disillusioned and retreated to singing opera in order to keep living.

The second bookend was the conflicts in the Balkans. Within just months of the collapse of communism in much of Europe, a war of succession in Yugoslavia surfaced. The sinister Slobodan Milosevic, President of Serbia, along with the Croatian leader Franjo Tudman, inaugurated a brutal program of genocide against the Muslim population. The atrocities were innumerable. Recently, the Russian invasion of the Ukraine would seem to seal the end of the era of the Cold War.

Other conflicts arose which put into question the perfect miracle of the miracle year. The most alarming was the Islamic State in Iran, which arose after the revolution in 1977 and transformed a vaguely liberal capitalist country into a theocracy. The rise of Isalmism coincided with this timetable, and Iran began research toward a nuclear weapon. President George Bush declared it "the axis of evil" along with Iraq and North Korea.

Other challenges continue to face Europe. One of the most dramatic is migration. Displaced Persons (DPs) may be the greatest tragedy of our time.[8] Since 2015, millions have fled their countries and sought refuge in Western

Europe. This has provoked fierce debates on human rights and host coun-tries.[9] For many historians, the migrations are nearly entirely negative—that is, people are fleeing from conflict and hardship. However, instead of a healthy discussion of rights we witness fierce debates on health and security. Bulgarian political scientist Ivan Krastev provocatively states that the refu-gee crisis has become Europe's 9/11, since it has unsettled what appeared to be an established order.

In one of her always thoughtful web reports, Judy Dempsy asked in 2019 whether post-1989 Europe was again building walls.[10] A panel of experts chimed in to answer, almost all in the affirmative. Ian Bond, director of foreign policy at the Center for European Reform, asserts the commonly held view that unlike the Cold War barriers, which were meant to keep people in, the new walls are designed to keep people away from Europe: "The walls (actual or metaphorical) that Europeans are putting up now, by contrast, are designed to keep people out, and to stop them sharing in our peace, prosperity, and good fortune. Instead of welcoming those who want to share in our freedoms, more often than not we now fear them and prefer to exclude them."

Perhaps the biggest challenge is one of a mood. Instead of the heady he-roics of 1989, life went back to "normal," where politics lost its "epic quality" (according to the *Washington Post*) in the absence of heroic stands against "evil empires."[11] Has any progress been made? Niall Ferguson notes, "Thus was the supposed triumph of the West in 1989 revealed to be an illusion."[12] Paul Betts claims we are returning to "the repressed" and the "narcissism of minor differences."[13] I don't think it is quite that bad. Betts himself is not entirely pessimistic, as his book *Ruin and Renewal* demonstrates.[14] Yet by any measure we are far away from the exhilaration of 1989.

So, where are we today? Can we move forward despite the confusion just described? It's hard to say. One of the insights of Timothy Keller, to whom this essay is lovingly dedicated, is that, unless one's belief is truly rooted in a transcendent God, the abandonment of one ideology only leads us to em-brace another. In his book *Counterfeit Gods*, Keller appraises the massive failure of communism around 1989.[15] So-called "scientific socialism" was a philosophy turned into an idol; belief in it came crashing down. Keller rightly asks what took the place of communism when that god fell. If it was market capitalism, it will prove as impotent as communism to solve problems like poverty and unhappiness. The reason? Our stubbornness in ignoring the side-effects of self-sufficiency.[16]

If progress is to be made, a few factors must not be overlooked. They are a call to Christians as well as to others.

1) It is easy to forget that one of the major contributing factors to the revolution of 1989 was from a Christian consciousness. Pope Jean Paul II with his media-savvy helped remind Europeans of their origins. His famous visit to Poland in 1979 saw him turn a political opportunity into a giant outdoor mass. The response was overwhelming. The labor movement Solidarity was largely driven by Roman Catholic sentiment. Even outside of Poland appeals to national identity are often admixed with a Christian consciousness.

Today we are far more secularized than in 1989. This subject is vast, and incapable of treatment in these few words. But Christians should know that human beings are innately religious. Europeans are often skeptical on the surface, yet they will respond to different options, as long as they are well-expressed religions.[17] One example of this is Russia. James Billington, former Librarian of Congress has studied and written extensively on Russia, its long history and culture. In his book *Russia in Search of Itself*, he ponders the future of Russia after 1989, and says that we just do not know where this vast country is going. But he says most Russians are searching "for a transcendence to take them beyond what they have known in the past and are experiencing in the present."[18] The Russian story is unique, with its struggle with authority, its martyrs, its faltering relation to the Orthodox Church, yet it is instructive for non-Russians.

Historian Niall Ferguson assesses the strengths and weaknesses of "the West."[19] Without going into too much detail here, Ferguson offers six reasons for the ascendency of the West.[20] Several of them, particularly the work ethic, are nurtured by distinctly Christian (Protestant) motives.[21] While he duly examines the secularization of the West, he nevertheless argues that the West has enough capital that it will stay on top for yet a few more years. But in the end the "rivals," especially China, will overtake the West, unless it reinvigorates its values. "Today, as then [1938] the biggest threat to Western civilization is posed not by other civilizations, but by our own pusillanimity—and the historical ignorance that feeds it."[22]

France is officially a laicized state (État *laïc*), espousing the revolutionary slogan, "liberty, equality, fraternity." But there are modest signs of hope. The Roman Catholic Church is experiencing a resurgence of interest in the faith, from two places: the Charismatic movement and the youth. Also, immigrant people arriving from the majority world tend to be practicing Christians (or Muslims). And the average French person has become quite fascinated with this religious fervor. This is hardly a revival, but it does mean the flame has not gone out. Other European countries have their own ambiguous history with the Christian faith. But in my judgment the future will not be good unless they sort this out.

2) The remarkable Vaclav Havel, upon becoming President of the Czech Republic, delivered a memorable New Year's Day address on January 2, 1990, in which he recognized the fragile nature of the new freedom from communism. Among other things he warned: "The great creative and spiritual potential of our nations is not being applied meaningfully. Entire branches of industry are producing things for which there is no demand while we are short of things we need."[23] He goes on to say that under communism the people became "morally ill" because they got used to saying one thing and thinking another. This led to utter skepticism. He continues: "We have learned not to believe in anything, not to care about each other, to worry only about ourselves."

The concepts of love, friendship, mercy, humility, or forgiveness have lost their depths and dimension, and for many of us they represent only some sort of psychological curiosity, or they appear as long-lost wanderers from faraway times, somewhat ludicrous in the era of computers and spaceships. Havel does not leave things there. He recognizes that despite this noose around the neck, the people—particularly the young people—found the strength to reverse the course. There was much suffering to get to this point. While not quite going all the way to proclaim the grace of God, Havel does remind his people that they will need to forgive and rediscover self-respect. Then this:

> Perhaps you are asking what kind of republic I am dreaming about. I will answer you: a republic that is independent, free, democratic, a republic with economic prosperity and also social justice, a humane republic that serves man and that for that reason also has the hope that man will serve it.

Where is Europe heading today? Indeed, where is the post-1989 geopolitical world heading? We do not know. Will we see an increase in authoritarian regimes, even Fascist-like resurgences? Is there anything left of the civic liberalism that characterized much of Europe for so many years? All of this is in God's hands. Will the people on our planet recognize their need for dependence on Him and on each other?

May the LORD answer you in the day of trouble!
May the name of the God of Jacob protect you!
May he send you help from the sanctuary
And give you support from Zion! (Psalm 20:1–2)

ENDNOTES

1   See Padraic Kenney, *A Carnival of Revolution: Central Europe, 1989.* (Princeton: Princeton University Press, 2002) esp. 23–56.

2   See the marvelous biography by Michael Zantovsky, *Havel: A Life* (New York: Grove, 2014). Havel remains one of the most compromised figures in history: a heavy smoker, unfaithful to his wife, and generally debauched human being. Despite this he emerged to assert the power of truth over against the reign of lies all around (and he did in his way eventually confess his sins and atone for his foibles).

3   Francis Fukuyama, *The End of History and the Last Man* (New York: Free Press, 2006, orig. pub. 1992).

4   Odd Arne Westad, *The Cold War: A World History* (New York: Basic Books, 2017).

5   Westad, *Cold War,* 627.

6   David Fromkin, "Nothing Behind the Wall," *New York Times,* November 7, 1999, https://www.nytimes.com/1999/11/07/opinion/nothing-behind-the-wall.html.

7   E.J. Dionne, Jr., "After the Cold War: A Healthy Normality," *Washington Post,* November 9, 1999, https://www.washingtonpost.com/archive/opinions/1999/11/09/after-the-cold-war-a-healthy-normality/f59c7a38-364c-4d07-9f34-6f6de5ce4e6b/.

8   See David Nasaw, *The Last Million: Europe's Displaced Persons from World War to Cold War* (New York: Penguin, 2020).

9   For a somewhat contrarian approach, see, Douglas Murray, *The Strange Death of Europe: Immigration, Identity, Islam* (London: Bloomsbury, 2017).

10 See Judy Dempsey, "Judy Asks: Is Post-1989 Europe Building Walls?", *Judy Dempsey's Strategic Europe,* November 7, 2019, https://carnegieeurope.eu/strategiceurope/80292.

11 E.J. Dionne, Jr., "After the Cold War," *Washington Post.*

12 Niall Ferguson, *The War of the World: Twentieth Century Conflict and the Descent of the West* (New York: Penguin, 2006), 638.

13 Paul Betts, "1989 at Thirty: A Recast Legacy" in *Past & Present* 244, issue 1, August 2019, 271–305.

14 Paul Betts, *Ruin and Renewal: Civilizing Europe after World War II* (New York: Basic Books, 2020).

15 Timothy Keller, *Counterfeit Gods: The Empty Promises of Money, Sex, and Power, and the Only Hope that Matters* (New York: Dutton, 2009) 104–106.

16 Keller, *Counterfeit Gods,* 107.

17 In *A Secular Age,* Charles Taylor thoughtfully comments that the West has not "subtracted" Christian faith but "added" to it with multiple options. (Cambridge: Belknap, 2018).

18 James H. Billington, *Russia in Search of Itself* (Washington, DC: Woodrow Wilson Center Press; Baltimore & London: The Johns Hopkins University Press, 2004), 149.

19 See especially Niall Ferguson, *Civilization: The West and the Rest* (New York: Penguin, 2011).

20 They are competition, science, property rights, medicine, the consumer society, and the work ethic.

21 Ferguson, *Civilization,* 256–294.

22 Ferguson, 325.

23 Excerpts from this speech may be accessed here: https://www.nytimes.com/1990/01/02/world/upheaval-in-the-east-havel-s-vision-excerpts-from-speech-by-the-czech-president.html.

NED **BUSTARD**

Creativity

THE HEIRS OF BEZALEL

Most people have a secret dream, a far-fetched vision that they keep tucked away in a hidden room in their hearts. Some may long to be a famous singer. Others might long to travel around the world or to be the monarch of an important nation. Fame, money, power—these all are rolled into one in my ridiculous fantasy. If you were to catch me in reverie, I would most likely be planning and organizing The Square Halo Museum—a beautiful collection of contemporary art inspired by the Christian faith.

In 2013 my good friend Dr. Robert Bigley was tasked with starting a performing arts center in our city, in the empty husk of the Lancaster Trust Company.[1] He said to me, "I can't give you a museum, but how would you like to have an art gallery?" I must have confessed my vision for The Square Halo Museum to him one night over a bottle of wine with our wives. Regardless of how he found out, I lost no time in giving him my reply: I immediately accepted his offer, and my first exhibition of art went up even before the doors to the rest of The Trust Performing Arts Center[2] had opened. The inaugural show of the Square Halo Gallery featured art by a number of the artists from *It Was Good: Making Art to the Glory of God*. Since then, I have averaged a new show every other month, showcasing a wide variety of artists—both living and dead, famous and should-be-famous.[3]

Square Halo Gallery is in the middle of downtown Lancaster and in the middle of the arts district—a block from "Gallery Row" and The Fulton Opera House.[4] Over time I found that the gallery was also in the middle of an aesthetic and theological no man's land. Of the Christians who entered the gallery, assuming it was a "safe" place for their tribe, many found that the art they considered "too modern" made them uncomfortable. And of the non-Christians who came in believing that the gallery—like any other downtown art gallery—was a "safe" place for their tribe, many were made uncomfortable by art they considered "too religious." This led me to eventually realize that my role as a curator and gallery director is actually that of a translator—explaining contemporary art to the church, and explaining the Christian faith to the unchurched. I have come to appreciate that the calling of the Square Halo Gallery is to be neither a fancy museum or a cooler-than-thou moneymaking gallery, but to be a place to educate and beautify the city for God.

The apostle John also had a dream, a far-fetched vision we now call the Book of Revelation. In it he saw a glorious New Creation and the city of God that defies description. That city has been the plan since the beginning. When God gave mankind the cultural mandate at the dawn of Time, He was calling us to be city builders. "Cities are the 'culture-forming wombs' of the society, made by God to be so."[5] Cities are places for building, making, and growing. In cities people come to work together, live together, and blossom together. Business, justice, science, architecture, and the arts find a place to grow in these "wombs of society." Aesthetician Calvin Seerveld says,

> The reach of God's rule, the city of God—Augustine's *civitas Dei*—involves government, commerce, education, media, families, transportation, hospitals, organized sports, centers of art—all societal institutions. God's city is the place where God's will is to be done and cultivated as a tangible signpost on earth of the rule of God currently in place at God's throne, which sinless "city of God" Jesus will bring fully to earth at the end.[6]

Seerveld has also observed that the biblical vision of the city of God is distinct from but related to the church, therefore charting "a wide open terrain for Christians in the visual arts. This biblical perspective helps prevent us from assuming 'church art' or 'liturgical art' is the primary model for Christians in the visual arts."[7]

Should Christians be involved in growing cities? Tim Keller says that the "single most effective way for Christians to 'reach' the US would be for 25% of them to move to two or three of the largest cities and stay there for three generations."[8] In fact, Keller insists that "We can't not be involved in shaping culture."[9] If this is so, what vision could we embrace to help us work towards cultural transformation? Keller writes:

For a possible model, think about the monks in the Middle Ages, who moved out through pagan Europe, inventing and establishing academies, universities, and hospitals. They transformed local economies and cared for the weak through these new institutions. They didn't set out to take control of a pagan culture. They let the gospel change how they did their work—which meant they worked for others rather than for themselves. Christians today should strive to be a community that lives out this same kind of dynamic, which will bring the same kind of result.[10]

Before founding the Square Halo Gallery I tried to follow the model of the monks and set up a gallery in the narthex of our church. Our congregation included an unusual number of artists for a Presbyterian church at that time, but that venture only lasted for several shows—it was closed down after some members told the leadership that they wanted to go to church, "not to an art museum." My brothers and sisters did not understand that our calling to creativity was woven into our DNA in the Garden of Eden. This was disheartening, but it helped to prepare me for the educational aspect of the Square Halo Gallery's calling to the city for God. Therefore, much of the work I do is to communicate to the church that "being made in God's image means—it must mean—that human beings reflect in some way God's creative work."[11] I find myself frequently reminding them that the first record of God filling a human with His Spirit is when the artist Bezalel is set apart for artmaking. (Ex. 31:1–6) Often I need to repeat Leland Ryken's affirmation that the "The Bible endorses the arts ... [and] there is no prescribed style or content for art. God-glorifying art can be realistic or fantastic, representational or symbolic or abstract."[12] But the educational calling of my gallery occurs at both ends of the spectrum. For example, I have had visitors come in to the gallery and ask "Why does that man have holes in his hands and feet?"—demonstrating the illiteracy of my community concerning even the basics of the gospel. And even the most rudimentary of Sunday School stories—Noah's Ark, Daniel in the Lion's Den, and Jonah and the Great Fish—are unknown to many who step through our doors on a First Friday.

One of the earliest titles from Square Halo Books is *It Was Good: Making Art to the Glory of God,* a book I contributed to and edited. Over the years I have found that, if by chance someone has heard of the book, it is usually because they read a quote from it by Tim Keller. In his essay for *It Was Good* he asserts that Christianity needs artists because "we can't understand truth without art."[13] The transcendentals of Goodness, Truth, and Beauty are so organically intertwined with one another that to we need beauty to pull truth from our heads to our hearts. Keller wrote that

> Art is a natural vehicle for pouring out the praise we long to give God. Without art it is almost impossible to praise God because we have no means by which to get the praise out. We can't enjoy God without art. And even those of us who are terrible artists have to sing sometimes.[14]

And so, as my gallery has grown, a calling equal—if not greater—to that of education has emerged: that of getting God's praise out through beauty. It has been a delight to watch parched souls come in and drink with wonder (and amazement) from the wells of beauty they have found in the iridescent paintings of Makoto Fujimura, the gilded drawings of Sandra Bowden, the exotic prints of Sadao Watanabe, the scrumptious collages of Mary McCleary, and more. Real, honest beauty is such a rare thing in our society that to see it in person often produces a profound, indescribable experience in the hearts of my gallery's guests.

The impact beauty has on people is not a rare or debatable phenomenon. We are not surprised when people are moved beyond words by the sight of the mysterious Giant's Causeway, the majestic California Redwoods trees, the epic Grand Canyon, the lush Great Reef, or the massive Uluru. In fact, entire industries have grown up to take us to visit them. But because art is man-made, the visceral reaction it can generate often catches us off guard. We need not be flabbergasted, for "At its best, art is able to ... satisfy our deep longing for beauty and communicate profound spiritual, intellectual, and emotional truth about the world that God has made for his glory."[15] When we are swept up into the glory of natural or man-made beauty, we are, in a sense, returning to the creation of our entire reality that is described in Genesis. For, as poet Malcom Guite reminds us, "at every moment in which we are conscious and perceive God's world, God is *in that same moment* creating it."[16]

Every human has been made in the image of God; we are by design creative beings. The artmaking of both the atheist and the follower of Christ is worth considering as praiseworthy because "all art and all creativity declares His glory, even apart from the content or the intent of the artist. As Author and Originator of all creativity, His signature is written on the creative act itself."[17] Of course, Paul wrote, "test everything; hold fast what is good" (1 Thess. 5:21), and the apologist Francis Schaeffer warned that "not every creation is great art ... So, while creativity is a good thing in itself, it does not mean that everything that comes out of man's creativity is good."[18] That caveat for our fallen nature acknowledged, it is important that we seek out and encourage "artists to stimulate that imagination and to show us that things have meaning," as Keller writes, because "Artists have a special capacity to recognize the 'other country' and communicate with the rest of us regarding the greater reality. A good artist will reveal something about the greater reality in an indefinable but inescapable way."[19] Calvin Seerveld explains some of how this is when he writes that,

> God's Spirit calls an artist to help her neighbors who are imaginatively handicapped, who do not notice the fifteen different hues of green outside the window, who have never sensed the bravery in bashfulness or seen how lovely an ugly person can be—to open up such neighbors to the wonder of God's creatures, their historical misery and glory.[20]

As an artist growing up in the church, I have a seen a great deal of growth in my brothers and sisters as they are beginning to see the value and need for creativity and the arts in the lives and work of believers. There has been a shift from hostility toward aesthetics, to a conversation about if a Christian can be an artist, to an affirmation of the calling of Christians to the arts. There was a time when a book on art and faith was harder to find than a needle in a haystack. Now, I have entire shelves of books in my studio addressing the topic and showcasing art made by my fellow Christians. Thankfully, there is a context now in many corners of the church that makes it possible to imagine groups of people reading our *It Was Good*[21] books and having lively discussions around the ideas presented in those myriad of essays. It is far more rare now to find a lone artist struggling with the awkward question "Am I a Christian artist or an artist who is a Christian?" Now it is much more common to find followers of Christ who are confidently living out their artistic callings and feeling no dissonance between that work and the Christian life.[22]

It has been exciting to see the church embrace creativity and the arts more and more over the past few decades, but recently I have realized that there is a potential side effect to this growth. I think it first hit me about five years ago while pulling prints with Brent Good, an old friend and a talented art professor at Messiah University. As we were discussing various and sundry things, I mentioned that I believed that among artists who claimed

Christ, in the wake of the needed abandonment of the concept of "Christian artist" there seemed to have been an almost gnostic adoption of an identity as an artist that had no relationship at all with our identity in Christ. It is as if Christians have been released from a big gray cube of Christian fundamentalism to then run and lock themselves in a big white cube of Art World fundamentalism. Rather than following a third way of reveling in the amazing freedom we have as redeemed image bearers to make art to the glory of God, I was worried that the heirs of Bezalel were going to squeeze into the mold of the mainstream.

I had almost recanted of my doom-and-gloom prophecy about the state of artists of faith when I came across an observation by Jeremy Begbie in *A Peculiar Orthodoxy: Reflections on Theology and the Arts*. In that book he wrote:

> If I had reservations about the present-day scene, they would not concern the liveliness of the field or its seriousness or depth ... but what often seems to be lacking is the sustained exercise of what some have called a "scriptural imagination."[23]

If Begbie is right, we have navigated clear from the Scylla of awkward Jesus-junk artmaking but have been shipwrecked by the Charybdis of cauterizing the Spirit when we are in the studio. And I would testify that among artists of faith there seems to be a lot of imagination, but not necessarily *scriptural* imagination. Begbie describes scriptural imagination as being "a sustained immersion" in the Bible paired with an embrace of classic creedal traditions.[24] Becoming rooted in God's word would help us to live faithfully to the call of Christ on our lives; being rooted in a solid creedal tradition would help focus and energize a scriptural imagination.

Keller would not be surprised by the kind of pendulum swing I was worried about and which Begbie describes. In fact, he has already written about it:

> Christians make two opposing mistakes in addressing the idols of their vocational field. On the one hand, they may seal off their faith from their work, laboring according to the same values and practices that everyone else uses; on the other hand, they may loudly and clumsily declare their Christian faith to their coworkers, often without showing any grace and wisdom in the way they relate to people on the job.[25]

We do not need savvy christian *Artists* siloed off from the faith, nor do we need saccharine *Christian* artists siloed off from the world. We need true *Christian-Artists* who have the vision and desire to look for a third way. We need Christians who understand that "spiritually-charged creativity comes from the sanctuary of a life hidden within God"[26] and who therefore invest time and resources to root themselves in the gories and glories of that Story of a magnificent King who died to save His kingdom. We need Christians who live their lives with the chosen people of the New Creation. Certainly the third way is not an easy path to follow. Both the big gray cube and the big white cube are more comfortable in their own ways. But Exodus 31 tells us that God filled Bezalel with *both* the "ability and intelligence, with knowledge and all craftsmanship, to devise artistic designs, to work in gold, silver, and bronze, in cutting stones for setting, and in carving wood, to work in every craft" *and* with His Spirit (vv. 3–5).[27]

Author Heidi Johnston offers these strong words of help and vision for the need for (and value in) a life of scriptural imagination:

> If the things we write or create are to offer hope and meaning then they must be rooted in truth. We need the anchor of Scripture, not only to bring meaning to what we create, but also to stop us losing sight of the tale we are telling.... When we speak purely out of our own imaginations our words do little to penetrate the darkness, however hopeful they may seem. Only when we are anchored in what is true can we find the freedom to wrestle with life's big questions without becoming despondent, to explore beauty without becoming hedonists, and to enjoy the privilege of intimacy with God without losing sight of who He truly is.[28]

I love the work of education and beautification the Square Halo Gallery does for the good of our city and the glory of God, and I still have a dream of seeing it become a full museum. But I have an even more glorious vision now—to see artists who follow Jesus be inspired by the creeds of His church and anchored in the strange and glorious Story our Creator is spinning. I long to see artists who, like Bezalel, are highly skilled and filled with the Spirit of God, making imaginative art that "goes beyond what we can think of and rises to lofty heights where it contemplates the glory of God."[29]

ENDNOTES

1   In 1912, Lancaster's largest bank, the Lancaster Trust Company, finished construction on its new downtown headquarters. Sparing no expense in the process, the Lancaster Trust Company built one of the region's most stunning buildings, a Beaux-Arts masterpiece from the imagination of Lancaster's leading architect, C. Emlen Urban. A century later, Mr. Urban's architectural treasure was re-imagined as The Trust Performing Arts Center.

2   In 2013 The Trust Performing Arts Center (https://www.lancastertrust.com) was established to honor God by encouraging excellence in the work of student and professional artists and by enriching our community through inspiring, challenging, and redemptive experiences. "Trust in the Lord, and do good; dwell in the land and befriend faithfulness" (Ps. 37:3).

3   Some of the artists I have had the honor to feature in my gallery include: Mary McCleary, Sandra Bowden, Guy Chase, Marc Chagall, Matthew Clark, Ruth Naomi Floyd, Makoto Fujimura, Daniel Finch, Jimmy Abegg, Mark Potter, Ryan Stander, Sadao Watanabe, Caleb Stoltzfus, Christine and Donald Forsythe, Wayne Adams, Steve Prince, Najwan Sack, Stephanie Lael Barrick, Brent Good, Craig Hawkins, Matt Stemler, Edward Knippers, and Georges Rouault. To learn more, visit https://www.squarehalobooks.com/sq-gallery/.

4   The Fulton Opera House, also known as the Fulton Theatre or simply The Fulton, is said to be the oldest working theatre in the United States. It was designated a National Historic Landmark in 1964.

5   Timothy Keller, "A Theology of Cities," *CruPress Green,* accessed January 15, 2022, https://www.cru.org/content/dam/cru/legacy/2012/02/A_Theology_of_Cities.pdf.

6   Calvin Seerveld, "Helping Your Neighbor See Surprises: Advice to Recent Graduates," from *Contemporary Art and the Church: A Conversation Between Two Worlds,* ed. W. David O. Taylor and Taylor Worley (Downers Grove, IL: IVP Academic, 2017), 213.

7   Ibid.

8   Keller, "A Theology of Cities."

9   Timothy Keller, *Center Church: Doing Balanced, Gospel-Centered Ministry in Your City* (Grand Rapids, MI: Zondervan, 2012), Chapter 26.

10 Ibid.

11 Paul Buckley, "Genesis 1 and the Pattern of Our Lives" (sermon), October 20, 2019, Wheatland Presbyterian Church, Lancaster, PA.

12 Leland Ryken, *The Liberated Imagination: Thinking Christianly About the Arts* (Wheaton, IL: Harold Shaw, 1989), 62.

13 Tim Keller, "Why the Church Needs Artists," from *It Was Good: Making Art to the Glory of God,* ed. Ned Bustard (Baltimore, MD: Square Halo Books, 2007), 121.

14 Ibid.

15 Philip Graham Ryken, *Art for God's Sake: A Call to Recover the Arts* (Phillipsburg, NJ: P&R Publishing, 2006), 8.

16 Malcolm Guite, *Lifting the Veil: Imagination and the Kingdom of God* (Baltimore, MD: Square Halo Books, 2021), 56.

17 Stephen Roach with Ned Bustard, *Naming the Animals: An Invitation to Creativity* (Baltimore, MD: Square Halo Books, 2020), 10.

18 Schaeffer, Francis A., p.52

19 Keller, "Why the Church Needs Artists," *It Was Good,* 120.

20 Seerveld, "Helping Your Neighbor," 211.

21 These are *It Was Good: Making Art to the Glory of God, It Was Good: Making Music to the Glory of God,* and *It Was Good: Performing Arts to the Glory of God.* For those who would embrace such a course of study, it would be wise to first read *Naming the Animals: An Invitation to Creativity* as a primer before launching into the *It Was Good* series, as they assume a basic understanding of the ideas presented in that book.

22 A helpful organization for those who want support and encouragement to work as a Christian in the visual arts is CIVA (Christians in the Visual Arts). CIVA has been serving artists and the Church for over forty years, with members around the world, biannual conferences, and their publication, *SEEN Journal*. Learn more at CIVA.org.

23 Jeremy Begbie, *A Peculiar Orthodoxy: Reflections on Theology and the Arts* (Grand Rapids, MI: Baker Academic, 2018), iv.

24 Personally, I have found the Reformed branch of the church to provide me with rich "soil" for thinking and making as an artist. It was Francis Schaeffer's *Art and the Bible* that made it possible for me to understand and embrace the idea that I could be both an artist and a Christian. In his article "What's So Great About the PCA?", Tim Keller wrote, "The best systematic theologies … all grow out of the same basic Reformed theological soil. The richness of Reformed theology inevitably inspires vigorous evangelism *and* sound doctrine; subjective spiritual experience and the 'great objectivities' of the sacraments; building the church *and* serving in society; creative cultural engagement and rootedness in historic tradition" (June 2010, https://scottsauls.com/wp-content/uploads/2019/07/Whats-So-Great-About-the-PCA-Tim-Keller.pdf).

25 Keller, *Center Church,* Chapter 26..

26 Roach and Bustard, *Naming the Animals,* 78.

27 Irish poet Andrew Roycroft tells those in the arts that there is a necessity to "establish your ratios," being intentional to properly balance "the degree to which we feed our aesthetic appetite, and the degree to which we meet our spiritual needs." This advice is part of a list of four priorities Roycroft developed to help in establishing a good balance in his artmaking to the glory of God. They relate more to literature but can be applicable to all the arts. To read the full list in context, go to https://thinkingpastorally.com/2018/10/30/appreciating-the-arts-to-the-glory-of-god/.

28 Heidi Johnston, "The Sheer Face of Story (Why Writers Need an Anchor)," *The Rabbit Room,* December 14, 2017, https://rabbitroom.com/2017/12/the-sheer-face-of-story-why-writers-need-an-anchor/.

29 Keller, "Why the Church Needs Artists," *It Was Good,* 120.

Jazz

A GRACE SUPREME

It was in the early 1990s that I first began to hear Tim Keller's name and to see in print a seemingly unending stream of quotes attributed to him. It made sense that I would. I was an elder at Christ Community Church (CCC) in Franklin, Tennessee, where Scotty Smith was pastor. Like Scotty, Tim was a faithful Presbyterian Church in America (PCA) gospel steward.

But the similarities don't end with denominational affiliation. These pastors attracted musicians. This included the gifted faithful who each week provide the church with musical worship. More unusually, though, their teaching attracted the greatest musicians in the world across multiple genres, who were creating the songs the whole world sings. The evidence of this would fill books—and specifically books someone else will have to write.

My work here is to point my writing compass at the subject of the city so often referred to in Tim Keller's mission, teaching, and writing. I can't think of any musician more qualified to join me in this pursuit than the Grammy Award-winning bassist and composer, John Patitucci. Like Scotty Smith and Tim as PCA pastors, the similarities between John and myself don't end with our Grammys. Instead, they begin and end with what Bono called "all that you can't leave behind." That is, our relationship with Jesus and the fruit of our work as musicians. We will leave it up to Jesus to determine which, if any, of our music will travel with us into the promised new heavens and new earth.

Hopefully, some of the jazz will make it—a music both John and I have spent a lifetime creating. Jazz is the music of cities, just as the mission of Tim and Redeemer has been oriented to cities. John was born in Brooklyn and has lived the majority of his life in New York, not far from Manhattan where Redeemer took root. And in case you're not hip to it, every jazz-playing person dreams of performing in New York City—as Sinatra sang, if you can make it there you can make it anywhere.

It was a revelation when John heard Tim teach about the fact that the Apostle Paul chose to go to the cities, the centers of art, culture, and the exchange of ideas. In one of our conversations, John referred to Tim as virtuosic, having "a creative, God-given, improvisational gift that can reach into people's hearts and inspire them to the core of their soul." High praise from one virtuoso to another.

Like John, I've been enriched by the music of John Coltrane and inspired by the fact that his most successful record is the one where he brings his spiritual search into the public square, the city. So it's not surprising that, wholly apart from one another, we both created workshops and tributes to the late tenor saxophone giant.

Tim and John once held a forum, a public conversation about Coltrane and his life—about what it was like to be an artist, develop a God-given gift to the fullest, and do it all without making an idol of the gift. That night John joined Brian Blade, Jon Cowherd, and Joel Frahm to perform the spiritual music of Coltrane. An unforgettable night, of that I'm sure.

Neither John nor I feel the need to have Coltrane conform to our explicit Christian theology. We both believe, as John puts it, that "God is the author of all creation, creativity, and every artistic vision that is good and uplifting." And so it is that when we hear Coltrane and his *A Love Supreme,* we are blessed to experience his music and to know, in faith and afresh, the Supreme Love of Jesus. As students of Tim's teaching, we've experienced this same good outcome.

What follows is a set of riffs, a duet improvisation—two grateful men looking at grace through the eyes of linear time.

Charlie Peacock: The first time I heard Tim teach I was immediately struck with how clear and unhurried it was—something like the intellectual, imaginative version of the three-point sermon. And the focus on grace, something I was getting for the first time with Scotty Smith after we moved from California to Tennessee—and really, something I couldn't get enough of.

John Patitucci: That's right, Tim talks so much about the gratitude for grace being the fire that fuels our obedience and commitment to God. I was raised in the Catholic church, and for the first fifteen years of my life I was an altar boy. I was not taught about God's transformative grace and loving forgiveness. In books like *The Prodigal God,* and in many sermons, Tim articulated God's grace in a such a powerful and beautiful way. To paraphrase, "We are indeed more sinful than we could ever imagine *and* more loved and forgiven than we ever could dream of."

CP: Ha! Love it. Reminds me of Jack Miller's quote: "Cheer up church, you're worse off than you think."

JP: I also love Tim's quote on humility: "Humility isn't thinking less of yourself, it is thinking of yourself less."

CP: A good word to every successful musician, indeed. What a relief it is to be free from the endless soul-sucking endeavor of making a name for yourself! I might have thought I was chasing a career back in the day. Now I can see I was running after freedom—a freedom shalom. For a jazz musician, freedom is fuel. When grace informs our freedoms, we are truly free.

JP: Yes. The freedom that Christ brings in placing us in close community (where we truly get close and become vulnerable) makes it possible for us to grow, through joys and sorrows, into the absolute best version of what He intended us to be. In jazz, we eventually learn that individual expression alone will not sustain us or takes us to the "mountain top" highs of improvisational experience we hunger for. Only in the like-hearted group can you get to that "freedom thing" where everyone in the group serves each other in the moment, and the music can truly be transcendent for the musicians and the audience as well.

CP: For the good of the people and the places they reside—that's the mission isn't it? Neighbor love through jazz. For both of us, jazz in the city has grown into gospel in the city. This new way of being in Jesus affects every aspect of life—including jazz and city-making. Though jazz is quite young compared to city-making, a vast human enterprise with a long history. I'm thinking of the story of Babel. And there's Jericho, a city still on the map today, something like 9,600 years old. The influence of the deep past remains. We still create cities using the grid plan developed by the ancient Greeks. Just like you and me using the deep past of music history to create music future.

There's a powerful, cosmic relationship between us and the cities we build, right? Of all the creative work humanity has teased out of the earth, none compares to the city. We shape the city of our hopes and dreams, and then the city turns and shapes our dreams afresh and renews our hope. Or it doesn't. There is no neutrality. In the realm of twentieth-century American church planters, Tim was prescient and way out on the leading edge with respect to city-making. The city and its inhabitants were not a target for the gospel, but rather a people and place in which the gospel took root and flourished. Tim and those early Redeemer folks got that right.

JP: When my wife Sachi and I moved back to New York in 1996, we attended Redeemer Presbyterian. One Sunday, Tim spoke about a church

plant called Trinity Presbyterian in Westchester County and we felt led to
visit. We stayed and were involved in that church for almost twenty years.
There, we played all kinds of music with world-class musicians in the classical and jazz world, people like Larry Dutton from the Emerson String
Quartet. Occasionally, Sachi and I would play at the Redeemer services in
NYC as well, first with Tom Jennings, and later Jon Cowherd and the many
other fine musicians there.

CP: Yes, Redeemer was an embarrassment of musical riches. I played
and sang at a service there with Tom Jennings, and it was inspiring to see
and hear such world-class musicians serving the church. I can truly say
that following Christ has helped me be the best musician I can be. Now
forty years in, I can't imagine what a life in music would look like without
close proximity to Jesus. I suspect you feel the same. I wish every musician I
know could enjoy the mission and meaning of following Jesus as a working
musician. In all your travels and amazing bands you've been in, what is the
one thing that musicians consistently get wrong about Christianity that
you wish they'd get right? I'd love to know.

JP: First, there's the issue of the musician putting individual expression above everything else—what we'd call making music an idol. There
simply is no room in their heart for Jesus. Music and self are taking up
all the space. Second, there's still a general misunderstanding in Christian
culture about the use and enjoyment of music. Musicians pick up on these
erroneous notions and naturally reject them, and often bristle when spoken to about faith in Christ.

CP: I get that. I wrote a whole book about it to work out my frustrations!

JP: I remember a time in the late 1980s, when I started making my own
recordings as a leader with my own compositions. Some fellow Christians
asked me, "When are you going to make a record for the Lord?" I was so
frustrated by that remark, because I subscribed to the same view as Bach.
He wrote *Soli Deo Gloria* on all of his scores, indicating that every note
that he wrote was for the glory of God. That's exactly what I believed I was
doing. I have heard many stories of musicians who were told that they
should never play their music outside of church, in the world. The Bible
never speaks about a separate Christian world. I always thought, we were
to be "in the world, but not of it."

CP: Yes, and with respect to Tim Keller and Redeemer, in the city, but not of anything that is anti-human, anti-peace, or anti-good. I so wish that my musician friends who have yet to follow Christ knew how free I feel as a disciple of Jesus, how free I feel to explore any music anywhere.

JP: Sadly, many musicians wind up thinking that if they become a Christian, they'll lose their freedom and creative expression instead of finding it.

CP: But your witness is that you have found it. And amazingly, you've played and worked alongside the greatest musicians on the planet. It's not just jazz in the city for you, it's jazz in the world. Freedom in Christ has given the ultimate freedom to live for Jesus in every circumstance without buying into the idea that self-fulfillment is the ultimate goal. It's love though isn't it? That's your goal. And mine too. During the pandemic, you were kind enough to make a record with me—and I would add, brave enough to endure my idiosyncratic compositions. Thank you. If you're up for it, let's close with a tradition in jazz of what we call "trading fours." Ready?

CP: Grace.

JP: Love beyond measure.

CP: Social justice.

JP: A commandment often neglected.

CP: Gospel community.

JP: Necessary, a blessing, and a challenge.

CP: Cultural renewal.

JP: A needed inspirational and uplifting force for society.

CP: Church plant in the city.

JP: Exciting, frightening, growth-inducing, beautiful, and sometimes like the back side of Disneyland.

CP: Tim Keller.

JP: A man of God.

VOCATION

KATHERINE LEARY **ALSDORF**

Work

TRANSFORMED

In his most recent book, *Exiles on Mission: How Christians Can Thrive in a Post-Christian World,* Paul Williams makes an impassioned plea to see believers experience "the power of the Holy Spirit working through them in their workplaces and neighborhoods and in the public square."[1] He acknowledges the momentum of the faith and work movement over the last two decades, while bemoaning that church leaders and the theological academy continue to marginalize the movement and co-opt its energy, preferring to increase lay participation in the programs and ministries of the gathered church. Williams notes, however, that one rare exception is "Redeemer Presbyterian Church in New York City, under the leadership of Tim Keller, with its Center for Faith and Work," where the effort to engage and equip congregants for their working lives is regarded as essential to, rather than a distraction from, the real mission of the church.[2]

I had the privilege of working with Tim from 2002–2012 to establish and lead the Center for Faith & Work (CFW) and then help launch the Global Faith & Work Initiative at Redeemer City to City. Williams is correct in saying that this vocational discipleship focus has been central to the mission of Redeemer and transformative in the work lives of thousands. Furthermore, I'm now seeing the emphasis and the substance of Tim's vision for faith-full work in the city begin to shape and influence the broader faith and work movement in cities across North America and around the world.

In this essay I will describe some of the core ideas and values Tim contributed to my own vocational work as well as to the faith and work movement at large.

When the Kellers first came to NYC to start Redeemer Presbyterian Church in 1989, I was fully inoculated against the Christian faith and painfully absorbed in a demanding career. After seventy-hour weeks, I'd often ask myself,

"Is this all there is?" Eventually, in my hope for an easier path, I decided to pray to God. God didn't answer those prayers the way I'd hoped, but He did lead me to the Redeemer start-up church and its pastor, Tim Keller. Tim taught that our work mattered to God and that caught my attention! Over time I came to believe that what the Bible has to say about God and Jesus is true and good, even if I couldn't yet figure out what that might mean for my work in the world.

This was early in a three-decade NYC explosion of growth in jobs, industries, wealth, and transplanted young adults seeking successful careers. From the pulpit and in our leader training, Tim called us to be a missional church, contributing to peace, justice, and flourishing in the city.[3] He encouraged us to *be the church* both when we are gathered together for worship *and* when we are scattered throughout the city in our neighborhoods and places of work.[4] The goal of salvation, he taught, is not solely a right relationship with God and a ticket to live in heaven forever, but the re-creation of the whole material world. He challenged us to start right where God had placed us, in our jobs in NYC. Over those three decades, the city grew, and Redeemer, with that message to hungry young adults, grew along with it.

But what did "being missional" in our places of work look like? What might it look like to integrate a gospel-centered faith with a career and life in NYC, a place where the vestiges of a Christian society were actively being rejected? NYC—the place where "making it" meant you could "make it anywhere"?[5]

These questions became more urgent and daunting for me when I was unexpectedly moved into the role of company president. I'd come to believe it was God's leading, but I hardly felt up to the task—leading a tech company and doing it distinctively as a Christian. That role led to running a startup tech company in Europe and then becoming CEO of two more tech companies in Silicon Valley. My faith grew along the way, but it was on-the-job training. My local churches were not very helpful; I listened to Tim Keller sermons on tape from a distance.

A decade after first accepting Christ at Redeemer and following these career advancements, I received an invitation from Redeemer to return to NYC to help start a faith and work ministry. My primary qualification for this totally unexpected career switch was my own frustration with how little churches were doing to equip their people for gospel-transformed, God-glorifying work in the world. Even the para-church ministries I'd seen seemed more moralistic than gospel-centered and better suited to the yesteryear of a predominantly Christian society. Redeemer was committing itself to establish a church-based faith and work ministry that equipped people to live out their lives wholly transformed by the gospel. In 2002 I accepted the invitation.

Early in the formation of CFW, I got to know David Miller, a scholar of the faith at work movement.[6] His research showed fragmented activity that had been largely lay-driven, isolated from church structures and the thought-leadership of seminaries and the academy. Churches were more focused on bringing people *into* the church than equipping them to be sent *out*. Many businesspeople and other workers were either choosing to keep their faith and their work distinct or just didn't know how to integrate them. He observed that various faith and work ministries had divergent orientations toward faith and work integration, which Miller categorized as follows:

Evangelism—focusing on introducing others to Jesus; seeing the workplace primarily as a mission field for evangelism, thereby living out the Great Commission.

Ethics—attending to personal virtue, business ethics— "an emphasis on discerning right action and ethical behavior in the marketplace and developing business practices and leadership styles modeled on biblical principles and people."[7]

Experience—addressing questions of vocation, calling, meaning, and purpose in work; recognizing that work has a larger role of serving greater societal purposes and needs.

Enrichment—looking to the resources of the faith to provide encouragement, healing, and sustenance to meet the challenges of work.

It seemed to me that, in order to lean into Tim's vision for faith and work ministry, CFW would need to be oriented to all four of these areas and go deeper still.

It didn't take long to uncover the pent-up demand for faith and work conversations within the Redeemer church community. As a largely young and educated congregation, people were struggling with many things in their work lives: the demands of their jobs were excessive and they had no "life"; they didn't know any other Christians in their company or field; they didn't see how what they did every day could possibly matter to God; and they often didn't know how to pray regarding their work. I could have led a class on Vocational Decision Making (or Calling) every week of the year and it would have always been full.

Over time, Redeemer's CFW would establish a wide range of programs to equip, connect, and mobilize the church community for gospel-centered work in the world, including:

Vocation Groups—we supported leaders in at least fifteen different vocations to pull together others in their field, on a monthly basis, to discuss shared challenges, wrestle with helpful Scripture and theology, and deepen their understanding of how God might be leading them.

Classes and Intensive Discipleship—we led five- and seven-week classes that addressed topics of interest, such as: God's plan for work and the problem of work, character and virtue in a post-Christian world, employee/employer relationships, knowing whether to quit or to stay, and servant leadership.

In 2008, with the goal of going deeper, we launched a nine-month intensive Fellowship program[8] to create learning communities committed to gospel transformation in all aspects of their work lives. That program—The Gotham Fellowship—continues today, has organically spread to churches around the world, and has more than 1,500 alumni worldwide.

Arts Ministries and Programs—We had monthly fellowships, classes, art shows and auctions, dance performances, and a literary journal to disciple and encourage the many artists in our midst.

Entrepreneurship—CFW pioneered an Entrepreneurship Initiative to encourage entrepreneurs at the idea stage of a new venture and help them think redemptively about every aspect of their venture—from its purpose, to organizational culture and practices, to stewardship of funding, people, and relationships. An annual business plan competition and conference were highlights of this ministry, launching dozens of ventures that continue to this day.

Conferences and Lectures—We also hosted larger annual conferences and lectures to feature thought leaders in various fields.

While the programs drew wide participation and many committed leaders, the programs themselves were secondary to our desire to help people experience spiritual transformation based on a deeper understanding of God and the gospel.

One of the most significant contributions that Tim Keller and Redeemer have made to the faith and work movement, as well as to my own life and work, has been this focus on the gospel and how it changes everything. "The gospel is not about something we do but about what has been done for us, and yet the gospel results in a whole new way of life."[9] The gospel is the means by which everything is renewed and transformed by Christ—be it a heart, a relationship, a church, a community, an organization, or a city. All our problems come from a lack of grounding in the gospel.[10] Put simply: the gospel transforms everything—our hearts, our thinking and how we work!

GOSPEL-TRANSFORMED WORKERS

Tim Keller's focus has been that we shouldn't think about the Christian life as a set of rules, but should ask instead, "What is the way that is in-line with the gospel?"[11] As Paul says in his confrontation with Peter, "We...know that a man is not justified by the works of the law, but by faith in Jesus Christ. So we, too, have put our faith in Christ Jesus that we may be justified by faith in Christ and not by the works of the law, because by the works of the law, no one will be justified" (Gal. 2:11–16 NIV).

One of our jobs at CFW has been to help people move from religion (legalism) or irreligion (license) into a relationship with Jesus. We tried not to give answers to questions like:

- Should I or should I not work on Sunday when my boss asks me to?
- My company wants to invest in a company that I think is immoral. Should I quit?

The Bible is not primarily about how to live right. It's not a set of rules. It's about a Savior. In both religion and irreligion, people seek to be their own saviors and lords. We want people to see that both their sins and their good deeds can be ways of avoiding Jesus as Savior. To "get" the gospel is to turn away from self-justification and instead rely on Jesus' record for a life-giving relationship with God.[12] We are not reconciled to God through our efforts and record but through Christ's work on the cross.

So my response to the questions above is usually, "It depends." Our response to the gospel may lead us into broken situations as Christ's ambassadors, not to demonstrate our own self-righteousness but to humbly seek to serve others.

Our work life reveals a Pandora's box of idolatries.[13] Martin Luther defined idolatry as looking to some created thing to give what only God can give. We may struggle with ambition, jealousy, pride, insecurity, control, and lack of discipline. Work may bring out the rebel or cynic in us. It may foster self-righteousness and self-esteem. In all cases, God's grace, love, and sovereignty are lost as we strive to be our own saviors. We all tend to hide or minimize our faults, mistakes and selfishness in order to look good in the eyes of the world. This gets to the heart of the gospel-transformed worker.

As Christians, it's important to recognize the depth of our own sinful nature in order for Christ's payment on the cross to excite and transform us. Understanding the redemption accomplished by Christ's life and death enables us to acknowledge our sin without it crushing us or causing us to deny or repress it. Take away either the knowledge of sin or the knowledge of grace and people's lives are not changed.

One of the most rewarding parts of the faith and work ministry has been to see people freed from the burden of covering up or repressing their own weakness and brokenness and then experience work as a calling and gift from God. The gospel provides the means to confess our selfishness, fears, and idolatry to God who sent His Son to rescue us. The good news is that the Holy Spirit works through our repentance and changes our hearts such that we want to serve God and the people He's placed in our lives. Tim Keller often quoted one of his mentors, Jack Miller, as saying, "Cheer up! You're a worse sinner than you ever dared imagine. Cheer up! You're more loved than you ever dared hope!"[14]

As gospel-transformed workers we can:

- develop more awareness of our own brokenness and selfishness and therefore become more humbly able to work with others, both Christian and non-Christian,
- focus less on what we can get from our work and engage more with what we can give to it,
- persevere under the toil and hardships of work because of Jesus' promise, "Come to me all you who are weary and burdened and I will give you rest ... For my yoke is easy and my burden is light" (Matt. 11:28, 30 NIV), and
- take God-honoring risks to our status, income, and security because our identity is in Christ and our trust is in His calling and provision.

Faith at work isn't just about our ethical behavior in the workplace or our witnessing to colleagues. Tim pointed us to the importance of the issues of the heart and the way we function as people alienated from God, which shapes our workplace behavior, decisions, and attitudes. Working from the inside out, there's good news—the gospel changes our hearts! The gospel is good news for the worker and good news for work.

As Dorothy Sayers says, "[Work] is, or it should be, the full expression of the worker's faculties, the thing in which he finds spiritual, mental, and bodily satisfaction, and the medium in which he offers himself to God."[15]

GOSPEL-TRANSFORMED INSTITUTIONS

Tim Keller also challenged the church to think through how the gospel might change the institutions in which we work. Salvation is more than something Jesus has provided to individuals to escape the brokenness of this world. The cultivating, rescuing, healing, restoring project that we learn about in Scripture also applies to the organizations and institutions of society. The gospel has a broader scope than individual salvation. God cares about the structures of society: our companies and organizations and institutions matter!

CFW seeks to explore ways God might use us to recognize the dignity of our colleagues, be ambassadors of justice in our organizational systems, and serve our customers with integrity. The corporation or institution itself has intrinsic worth.

Culturally, we are in a time of institutional crisis. Many workers view their organization as merely a platform for individual advancement with little attachment to the health or flourishing of the institution itself. With our "consumer" mentality we hop from one institution (or church) to another to find greener pastures. However, there are theological and pragmatic reasons why institutions matter to God and, therefore, are worthy of our commitment to serve and lead them.

In the creation story we learn that God put humankind in the garden "to work it and take care of it." Through the "cultural mandate," the people God created in His image are given the opportunity to fill the world with a flourishing human society (Gen. 1–2). As we say in *Every Good Endeavor*, a good definition of work is "rearranging the raw material of God's creation in such a way that it helps the world in general, and people in particular, thrive and flourish." God envisioned and is sovereign over the various spheres of culture, as well as the institutions within those spheres. Internally and externally, an organization is meant to reflect God's character.[16]

Nonetheless, institutions and industries and whole economies are corrupted by the fall. As God's image bearers who have been redeemed by the gospel, we are called to serve within these institutions as God's redemptive co-workers, seeking the renewal of the organization itself. This requires a deep faith in the good news that Christ has renewed all things. That faith and sense of purpose has made people better able to persevere and even find joy in the midst of the thorns and thistles of everyday work.

GOSPEL-TRANSFORMED WORLD

The gospel is also kingdom-centered. The church, meaning its people scattered throughout all vocations, is called to serve God and society through work. We enter into the brokenness of the world with a view toward redeeming and restoring particular spheres of God's created order, as stewards of that order. We enter in with humility, seeking God's grace to work in some way through our efforts. He is the one doing the transforming and renewing; He invites us to join Him through the ordinary things of our work and life.

Again, Tim Keller has made this theology accessible and helped expand the scope of faith-at-work thinking from individual ethics and witnessing relationships to culture-making in the world at large.

The biblical storyline provides the foundation for our engagement in the world around us. The simple storyline is:

God's kingdom (this world) was originally good in itself (Gen. 1–2),
it is fallen and marred by sin (Gen. 3), and
it will eventually be redeemed under Christ the healing, renewing,
    restoring king (Rom. 8:18–21).

In most of the geographies, vocations, and organizations in which we work, other views of reality have taken precedence. These tend to identify some "created thing" as the source of the problem with the world and some other "created thing" as our salvation—our hope for the world. Our Western culture, for example, has identified lack of education as a major source of the problems with the world; education, therefore, is the solution. Some view capitalism or Marxism as the cause of the problems with the world, so one or the other must go. Conservatives or liberals are the problem; one of these must go.

At CFW we are indebted to Al Wolters who writes, "As far as I can tell, the Bible is unique in its rejection of all attempts to either demonize some part of creation as the root of our problems or to idolize some part of creation as the solution."[17] Christianity says that the answer to the problem with this world is sin and the solution is Jesus. Without the gospel, you *will* make something besides the Lord into a savior and you *must* make something else into the enemy. Only the Christian worldview locates the problem with the world not in any one part or group of people in the world, but in sin itself. Sin runs through every good created thing, so we cannot simply divide the world into the good guys and the bad guys. And the Christian worldview locates the solution in God's grace and the promise of God's kingdom to come.

With that as a foundation, our ministry has engaged people to think through ways their work—or their organization, or their industry—contributes to both the flourishing and the brokenness of the world, and how it can be moved further in the direction of flourishing.

This was a particularly difficult assignment for many of our congregation who worked in the financial industry. Often their motivation for working in their field was monetary—to pay off college loans more quickly, provide an attractive lifestyle, or be able to give money to causes they believed in. They struggled to see God's bigger purpose for the work itself. Ironically, it was when the global economy went into crisis, in the financial meltdown of 2008, that those in finance began to understand how reforming the industry could contribute to human flourishing.

It's naïve and even dangerously arrogant to think that a few Christians in an institution can transform it from brokenness to flourishing. The key is that God is already doing His work of restraining, sustaining, and renewing in the midst of the problems of the world. He doesn't *need us* to fulfill His redemptive purposes, yet He *invites us* to join Him in the grand project. By the very act of calling us into a saving relationship with Him He is also calling us to work in a broken world.

Against a backdrop in which much of the Christian evangelical culture in the US is in crisis mode, Tim Keller has helped us understand that God is always at work. God doesn't work only through Christians to accomplish His purposes. One common question among people in the church who are at work in the world has been, "Why is it that there are people I work with who aren't believers, but who appear to be better people and do more good than many Christians I know?" The doctrine of Common Grace provides helpful insights. Tim Keller describes it thus: because of Common Grace, the works—the thoughts, contributions, cultural creations, science—of nonbelievers are never as bad as their wrong beliefs should make them; because of Total Depravity, the works—the thoughts, contributions, cultural creations, science—of believers are never as good as their right beliefs should make them.

Jesus said that God "causes his sun to rise on the evil and the good and sends rain on the righteous and the unrighteous" (Matt. 5:45 NIV). Keller elaborates, "God gives good gifts of wisdom, talent, beauty, and skill graciously, in completely unmerited ways. He casts them across the human-race like seed, in order to enrich, brighten and preserve the world. Far from being unfair, God's unmerited acts of blessings make life on earth much more bearable than it should be given the pervasive effects of sin on his creation."[18]

This has far-reaching implications for how believers approach their work. We can find common cause with those who don't know the gospel. It is humbling, healthily so, to recognize that God blesses many non-believers with talents, wisdom, and virtue that we don't have, to do good work we wish we could do. And we can be encouraged as we develop eyes to see the many ways God is at work, through those who know Him and those who don't, bringing beauty, healing, justice, love, and mercy into broken places. "If the glory of God is indeed in all the earth as Scripture testifies, the mission of the people of God is to 'name the glory,' to name the unknown-known god; [Acts 17:23] to speak of the glory that has come down in the person and work of Jesus Christ."[19]

It remains a mystery exactly where we are in our present moment along the journey of God's redemption and re-creation of His entire creation. But I do believe that Redeemer has equipped many believers to work in the world, in their specific vocations and callings, to be ambassadors of His truth, love, and grace. While Scripture tells us that the battle has been won and Satan has been defeated, we remain in the "already, but not yet." We're still in the biblical story of redemption—some steps forward and some steps back, but always with glimpses of God's sovereignty and love.

CONCLUSION

In 2012 I was privileged to assist Tim Keller in the writing of *Every Good Endeavor: Connecting Your Work to God's Work*. It's dedicated to the staff and volunteer leaders of Redeemer's Center for Faith & Work who helped our congregation see that their work matters to God. I have been humbled and filled with joy to witness how God has been at work through the church's commitment to deep faith and work integration. And I'm extremely grateful to Tim Keller for the theological grounding and practical support he has offered throughout. His commitment to equip and mobilize the church to love and serve the institutions and culture of the city has transformed the work lives of many people and given us glimpses of God's ongoing redemptive work. His respect for the work we do in the world has given us greater dignity as people made in God's image. His own personal humility and trust in God's sovereignty has helped us become more winsome ambassadors of God's kingdom.

Tim opened and closed *Every Good Endeavor* with a retelling of Tolkien's story, *Leaf by Niggle*. It's a fitting close here, as well. Niggle had a vision of a beautiful tree that he spent a long time attempting to paint, yet he never got it done to his satisfaction. But after his death,

Niggle is put on a train toward the mountains of the heavenly afterlife. At one point he hears two voices. One seems to be Justice, the severe voice, which says that Niggle wasted so much time and accomplished so little in life. But the other, gentler voice, which seems to be Mercy, counters that Niggle has chosen to sacrifice for others, knowing what he was doing. As a reward, when Niggle gets to the outskirts of the heavenly country, something catches his eye.[20]

He sees his tree, finished in all its glory, and knows that this is a gift! The message resonates with all of us. Few realize even a fraction of what we imagine accomplishing and everyone wants to make a difference in this life. "But that is beyond the control of any of us," Tim wrote.

If this life is all there is, then everything will eventually burn up in the death of the sun and no one will even be around to remember anything that has ever happened . . . all good endeavors, even the best, will come to naught. Unless there is God. If the God of the Bible exists . . . and this life is not the only life, then every good endeavor, even the simplest ones, pursued in response to God's calling, can matter forever."[21]

Thank you, Tim, for working with me to paint a leaf. We can only imagine what our cities and culture would be like if all churches equipped their people for redemptive work in a broken world. We can imagine a just economy, fueled by people who worked for the joy of good work, well done. We can imagine artists helping us transcend the broken reality of our fallen world. All of us at the Center for Faith & Work were able to paint a leaf or two of a beautiful tree. And our hearts have come to hope in Christ and the future world He has guaranteed. Thank you for leading us on the journey to work with passion and rest, knowing that our deepest desires for our earthly work will ultimately be fulfilled when we reach our true county, the new heavens and the new earth.

ENDNOTES

1   Paul S. Williams, *Exiles on Mission: How Christians Can Thrive in a Post-Christian World* (Grand Rapids, MI: Brazos Press, 2020), xi.

2   Williams, *Exiles on Mission,* 20.

3   Jeremiah 29:4–7 were foundational to the mission of the church in the city: "Seek the peace and prosperity of the city to which I have carried you into exile" (NIV).

4   Under the priesthood of all believers, we know that we are all ministers to God's people, responsible to make Him known to the world. Individual believers do not need a priest to come to God; no hierarchy exists between laity and pastor. The only things that makes believers qualified is that we are in Christ. The only thing that makes us able is that the Spirit of God dwells in us.

5   Lyric from Frank Sinatra's "New York, New York."

6   David W. Miller, *God at Work: The History and Promise of the Faith at Work Movement* (New York: Oxford University Press, 2007).

7   Miller, *God at Work,* 129.

8   For more information on the Gotham Fellowship, see https://faithandwork.com/gotham-fellowship.

9   Timothy Keller, *Center Church: Doing Balanced, Gospel-Centered Ministry in Your City* (Grand Rapids, MI: Zondervan, 2012), 30. 7 Center Church, p30

10 See *Center Church,* Chapter 1 for an in-depth discussion of gospel theology and gospel renewal. Most simply, the gospel is the good news that, through Christ, we have been rescued from our alienation from God and all the brokenness that's ensued, and we are invited to receive the accomplished (already, but not yet) redemption of the entire physical world.

11 *The Gospel-Transformed Heart,* Tim Keller, April 2008, p 1.

12 Tim Keller's book, *The Prodigal God : Recovering the Heart of the Christian Faith,* does an excellent job of explaining how both the younger (prodigal) and elder (obedient) sons in Jesus' parable of the Prodigal Son were living apart from their father's love. The younger squandered his inheritance and the elder thought he had earned it. The elder brother's resentment at the end of the parable separated him from his father's love. (New York: Riverhead, 2008)

13 *Counterfeit Gods: The Empty Promises of Money, Sex, and Power, and the Only Hope that Matters,* by Tim Keller, goes into depth on the idols of our heart as well as the cultural idols that shape our worldview (New York: Penguin, 2009).

14 C. John (Jack) Miller, founder of World Harvest Mission (now Serge), founding pastor of New Life Presbyterian Church in Glenside, PA, and former faculty at Westminster Theological Seminary. Quote found in numerous Sonship materials.

15 Dorothy L. Sayers, "Why Work?" in *Creed or Chaos?: Why Christians Must Choose Either Dogma or Disaster* (Great Britain: Jarrold and Sons, 1947), 55.

16 To explore this idea further, listen to "Liberty University and the Reality of Institutional Sin" with David French and Curtis Chang (*Good Faith* podcast, November 20, 2021, https://goodfaith.thedispatch.com/p/liberty-university-and-the-reality).

17 Albert M. Wolters, *Creation Regained: A Transforming View of the World* (Grand Rapids, MI: Eerdmans, 1985), 50.

18 Timothy Keller, "What is Common Grace?", *Gospel in Life,* November 30, 2010, https://gospelinlife.com/downloads/what-is-common-grace/.

19 Keller, "What is Common Grace?"

20 Timothy Keller with Katherine Leary Alsdorf, *Every Good Endeavor: Connecting Your Work to God's Work* (New York: Penguin, 2010), 12.

21 Keller and Alsdorf, *Every Good Endeavor,* 14.

Both/And

YES

No single person has shaped my life and ministry calling more than Tim Keller. For more than thirty years, Tim's singular focus on illuminating the magnanimous grace of Jesus for sinners in the gospel has formed me spiritually. His gift to me and thousands of other New Yorkers is not that he told us *what* to think or *what* to do, but that he equipped us through his preaching about *how* to think in line with the gospel. He taught us that Jesus is beautiful, the Scriptures are true, and that offering our lives as a holy sacrifice to God (Rom. 12:1) is the only suitable response to such wondrous love.

It seems like yesterday that Kathy Keller and I were cutting danishes in the basement of East 87th Street and I took my vows to be a part of the second member class of Redeemer Presbyterian Church. But it was 1989! To us, Dr. Keller was just "Tim" and Redeemer was home—they still are. I met my husband Tom in the third row, Tim married us, and we baptized and raised three children in the Redeemer community of New York City.

Tim boiled complex things down and communicated them powerfully. I'll never forget the day I first heard him say that there are two ways to avoid Jesus: one is by sinning; the other is by trying to be good.[1] I lived in the second camp and can attest: it's exhausting trying to be good. Though I intellectually understood that my relationship with God was based upon the finished work of Christ, until I sat under Tim's teaching, I had no idea that functionally, I was a moralist. That is, I was working to follow Christ on the strength of my own righteousness. No wonder I filled my life with so much striving! I made much of myself and little of God and worked to be "right" in all matters of faith. I was trying to please God, but I was avoiding Jesus in the process. Tim showed me that the way out was by repenting of my own righteousness.

TIM TAUGHT ME THAT JESUS IS BEAUTIFUL

Through Tim, Jesus became beautiful *to me*. His foundational teaching showed me that what blinded me to the wonders of God's grace and love were the countless ways I tried to distinguish myself as a Christian—the opposite of what God wanted. When I realized I would never outgrow my need for grace, I saw that sin, weakness, and need are the very things that compel me to treasure Jesus alone. By beholding God's glory in the face of Jesus, I transformed.

Tim introduced me to the real Jesus, the most compelling person I have ever known. When he did, I was free to fall in love with Him and learn to prize Him above all else. This only happened when I came to the end of myself and was crushed in spirit at seeing how greatly I had prized myself and rejected Jesus, who alone could get me out of that pit. This is when my heart (not just my mind) experienced the reality that Jesus is beautiful—the restorer of the broken-hearted. And that realization set me on a journey which will continue until I meet Christ face-to-face—a path of continually repenting and believing the gospel *for me*.

As Tim's teaching kindled the fire that wrought this change in my heart, the renewing power of the gospel slowly reshaped my service—and it's still doing so. Grace bids me to do little things with great love and forbids me to do great things with little love.[2] It frees me from the ruling power of fear and humbles me to walk alongside my neighbor as a fellow sinner in need of mercy. Grace beckons me to come away and be with God and compels me to take great risks. More than anything else, I want to love with knowledge and depth of insight, "For the love of Christ controls us [me], because we [I] have concluded this: that one has died for all, therefore all have died; and he died for all, that those who live might no longer live for themselves but for him who for their sake died and was raised" (2 Cor. 5:14–15).

AVAIL: AN OUTGROWTH OF JESUS' BEAUTY

Avail was born from this central teaching of Tim's: Jesus is beautiful, and He's the most beautiful to the brokenhearted. From the beginning, Avail has been centered on Redeemer's gospel-centered preaching and a heart cry for the Holy Spirit to animate His people to action. It was God's answer to the fervent prayers of seven Redeemer women—I was among them—in 1992. We saw that some of the most desperate, brokenhearted, and shame-filled people in our city were those facing unexpected pregnancy and those who have had an abortion. Instead of being loved no matter what, these heartbroken women were caught in an aggressive tug of war between two strident positions—lost in the middle, isolated in their moment of deepest despair. Judged and scorned, they felt the meaning of their whole lives reduced to one moment. We wanted to meet them at their point of need, on their terms, and *love them no matter what.* We knew we could not assume that the baby did not matter to the women and men unexpectedly pregnant, no matter what they chose.[3]

So in our work, we asked ourselves, "What does it mean to display Jesus' beauty and expansive grace to these women, men, and children—image bearers in a story of unexpected pregnancy or abortion loss?" We committed ourselves to love well and leave the results to God. Twenty-five years later, Avail has loved thousands and thousands of New Yorkers—no matter what. The vast majority of women and men who come to Avail believe abortion their best or only option. Through Avail's work with them, clients feel empowered with enough support and resources to consider all their options, and each year 73–78% of reporting clients ultimately choose to carry to term. Thousands have found freedom from grief and shame, which enables them to look at their future with confidence and hope.

Avail was birthed, in a sense, from one of Tim's greatest strengths: his ability to make lofty theological truths accessible, relatable, and practical. Biblical tenets are relevant not just in their most obvious applications, but also to current-day complex issues like abortion. They are beacons heralding a path forward, more important than ever in these contested spaces. I have sought to apply these biblical truths, every implication of gospel reality, into each aspect of Avail. Over time, they have simply become a way of seeing.[4]

YES: THE REALITY OF "BOTH/AND"

Hidden within the title of this book is a concept of Tim's that I view as one of his most radioactive. It's a play on words that perfectly befits celebrating Tim's gospel ministry: "A City for God." I picture Tim's quizzical expression, turned head, and self-effacing question, "Or is it: God for the City?" Answering his own rhetorical question, he would then assert, "Yes." The city is to be for God, in the most profound sense, and God is powerfully and incarnationally *for* the city (Jonah 4:11)—demonstrating it through us and our work. Tim's wisdom is rooted in his keen insight into the mysterious both/and of the kingdom of God.

At Avail, we live with the reality that we—and every client we work with—are more sinful that we would ever dare believe, and more loved than we'd ever dare hope. This both/and truth of the gospel message gives us the highest view of God's love and secures the most sober view of man's depravity. The gospel woos us to live lives of faith amid the seemingly inherent paradoxes that inhabit the Bible's greatest truths: Jesus is both Son of God and Son of Man; sinners are saints; image bearers are depraved; man sins and suffers; the last are first; do justice and love mercy. The most stunning of all: death works life.[5] *Yes,* evil is present and worse than we realized and also Jesus is real and undoes the worst evil of all.

This gospel paradox does two critical things. First, it imparts deep shalom[6] for the Christian, for how did we come to know Christ except by Him being our Savior and Lord? We each feel sin's weight within ("Wretched man that I am! Who will deliver me from this body of death?"—Rom. 7:24) but then exhale relief at God's assurance ("Thanks be to God through Jesus Christ our Lord!"—Rom. 7:25). Secondly, it equips us to live uniquely among our neighbors with winsome love and wisdom. Humbled by God's judgment, we fear Him alone. Accepted by God's grace, we rest in His love alone. This leaves us unafraid of truth and without need to assert our rightness. Instead, we engage with the most intractable problems of our time (even abortion) with confidence, creativity, and even joy, because our hope for ourselves and the world is God alone. *Yes,* God's peace is real *and also* we freely offer—without force—the realities of this peace to the world's needy and broken-hearted.

Living this "both/and" dynamic enables us to navigate life's complexities with courage. It doesn't mean compromising eternal truths for weak half-truths, but rather, refusing to shrink truth to match our comfort. Embracing the *yes* of seemingly contradictory biblical claims calls us to the highest view of God and Scripture—and the deepest faith in the power of God. We become free to see reality in all its beauty and ugliness and to rely on the Holy Spirit to empower us to lead a supernatural life with hope that transforms the world. Tim's consistent call to consider my assumptions and recognize false dichotomies helps me break the logjam so I can embrace God's mysteries, even in their seeming contradictions. So, at Avail we hold fast to the dynamic tensions at the heart of gospel truths and faithfully apply them to unexpected pregnancy and abortion loss. *Yes,* abortion goes against God's design, *and also* the one considering it is brokenhearted, adored by God, and in need of unconditional love. At Avail we occupy both sides of these biblical paradoxes simultaneously.[7]

SEEING PEOPLE, NOT *THROUGH* PEOPLE

When men and women believe that abortion is their best or only choice, there are *many* broken realities that compel this belief. Some of these have made the men and women victims, some present towering obstacles to carrying to term, and some flow out of a selfish heart. Reducing unexpected pregnancy to a simple moral framework exposes our tendency to look through people. That's what the Pharisees did. They were moralists: they rejected grace and failed the law. They looked through Jesus and missed salvation.[8] But Jesus is the Way (John 14:6), and we can't love people we don't see. In Jesus, we have the model for seeing all people—for embracing the *imago dei,* the image of God, in all people. Tim taught often on *imago dei* and helped us grasp this truth: from Jesus, we learn how to love others fully, in truth *and* grace.

Sabrina and Michael came to Avail under complicated circumstances. Michael had recently been the random victim of a violent crime that left him blind in both eyes, unable to work, and requiring round-the-clock care. Sabrina, Michael, and their two young sons were evicted from their apartment and began living in homeless shelters around the city. All they had left was their car, which they were in danger of losing because of the parking tickets Sabrina had accumulated while driving Michael around to agencies for disability services. When Sabrina found out she was expecting their third child, she sat next to her husband sobbing. For her, she faced two clear impossibilities: having another baby or having an abortion.

In this unexpected pregnancy Avail saw the *imago dei* in five people who needed protection. This couple was overcome by complex suffering resulting from sins against them and saw no way forward. How should we respond in the face of such difficulty? Out of a desire to protect the life of the unborn child, do we minimize the parents' fears? Do we leverage their vulnerability for moral suasion? Do we ignore the sons' needs for stable school placement? Do we pretend we have all the answers or that they don't actually have a choice? No. We dare not. Is God for the woman, the man, or the child? *Yes!*

Love forbids us from pitting the interests of the woman and man against those of the unborn child, and the life of the child against them. Love requires that we sit with the man and woman in the pain of unexpected and fearful circumstances, that we listen first. Love affirms that their lives and interests are intertwined with one another and the unborn child, that family is a blessing, that parenting is sacrificial. Reality presents overwhelming challenges *but also* holds forth unexpected hopes and possibilities. We help carry the pain, and this empowers clients to overcome the complexities that often compel them to feel that abortion is their only option. In Mark 5:24–34, we read of a woman who came to Jesus with a chronic illness—she had been bleeding for twelve years. Unclean, she was by law excluded from the temple (Lev. 15:25–27) and had grown accustomed to ostracism and alienation.

In her culture, illness was often believed to be a sign of sin, so she was likely seen as a sinner or rejected by God.[9] Trembling with fear, she went to see Jesus and touched His cloak. Jesus shocked everyone by stopping and attending: "Who touched me?" (Mark 5:30). He listened to her story and not only healed but dignified her by publicly restoring her to community life (Mark 5:34). This is our model.

After several weeks of advocacy meetings—and despite receiving the complicated diagnosis of placenta previa—Sabrina and Michael decided they wanted to carry to term. They enrolled in Avail's Equip parent-education program and received diapers, clothes, formula, a baby car seat, and more. We introduced them to the Sisters of Life, one of our faith-based partners ministering to clients' needs, and they provided the family with a full Christmas dinner—the first the family had ever eaten together. An Avail donor learned of their story and paid off their outstanding parking tickets so they wouldn't lose their car. We connected them to our city referral partners who helped them find a stable living situation. We answered Michael's questions about what Christian faith means in practice in a way that he found life-giving.

By recognizing the *imago dei* of all five members of this family—by seeing them and not *through* them—Avail was able to walk them into the palpable love of Jesus. "I love it here!" their oldest son exclaimed during one visit as Michael reached down and touched the carpet, trying to understand what so excited his son. "Things were looking down when I walked into Avail," Sabrina recalls. "Now whenever I leave, I feel like things are looking up." Baby Trevor is now eighteen months old, and mother, father, brothers, and child are flourishing.

Yes!

DRAWING NEAR INSTEAD OF REMAINING ALOOF

"We cannot pray for you if you are considering abortion," answered Esther's pastors in response to her panicked midnight phone call. The stinging rebuke left her reeling.

We moderns have come to believe that the people we meet in 2022 present more challenging circumstances than those Jesus encountered in first century Palestine. But this is not true. We see on every page of Matthew, Mark, Luke, and John what it means that grace and truth came through Jesus, and He gave us numerous models to follow. As Tim says, to love as Christ loves is simple but it asks everything of us.[10]

When Esther placed that phone call, she was truly desperate. She was a Christian, living independently, virtuous and saving herself for marriage. But one night and one misstep was enough to undo it all. She did not want to be pregnant "this way." She replayed her mistake over and over all night, crying, "Where was grace? Where was God?" The next morning, Esther did a random search online and found Avail. She set an appointment that would—along with others that followed—change the course of her life. Client advocates began to virtually minister the grace and compassion she needed. She called their words "oil over the scars of my sins." They encouraged her that whatever decision she made, she would be loved. She began sharing her deepest fears about becoming a single mother. Her father was incarcerated her entire childhood and her mother was a drug addict. She dreaded ending up with the same sad story—pregnant, abandoned, struggling to support a child. The thought of being unmarried tormented her. Fear is expensive, and because of it she proceeded and took the first abortion pill.

But gospel love is incarnational (John 1:14). We know we are more loved than we dared hope because Christ, the eternal Son of God, became man. He left His place of honor, identified with us by becoming sin, and took on the judgment of hell. There is no lower place He could have taken. The Lover gives up His place and moves *toward* the beloved. No one can love from far away.

To the sinful woman at the well, marked by shame, Jesus asked for help. He said, "Give me something to drink" (John 4:7). To Zaccheus in a tree, a traitor and thief, Jesus said, "Come down, I'm going to your house" (Luke 19:5). Jesus moved toward each sinner in a demeanor of welcome and even honor. He covered their shame. And they were overcome in their joy, bold in their proclamation of His goodness. "Come see the man who told me all I ever did? Could He be the Christ?" the woman said (John 4:29). "I will give back four times what I have stolen!" Zaccheus said (Luke 19:8). Jesus is the only person in human history who could justifiably have remained aloof from sinners, but He drew near. He didn't avoid this uncomfortable tension. Rather, He leaned into it.

We frequently see something very different in the ways the local church interacts with those unexpectedly pregnant or living in the wake of a past abortion. The Church zealously champions the unborn, but often it simultaneously remains aloof or even condemns the woman or man struggling with the weight of their situation. Nearly half of women (43%)[11] who choose termination were attending church at least once a month at the time of their abortion, and these women generally feel shame and isolation. We know this because only 7%[12] of them have discussed their decision to abort with someone from their local church. This begs the question: is the church more likely to approach these women in the spirit of the Pharisee ("God, I thank you that I am not like other men, extortioners, unjust, adulterers, or even like this tax collector"—Luke 18:11), than they are with the words of Jesus ("Let him who is without sin among you be the first to throw a stone at her"—John 8:7)?

The Church must be zealous about the unborn and the doctrine of life, but also zealous and proactive about the forgiveness Christ offers. It must be both these things, in equal measure. Our spirit of grace should match the one Jesus showed to the woman caught in adultery in her moment of public shame, saying, "I see you, I love you, I'm here with you." Sadly, because this is so rarely our response, many women and men choose to suffer in silence with the often debilitating consequences of abortion rather than endure the shame they fear they'd meet in their local church if they were honest. We may be zealous for truth and life, but are we also, as Tim asks, zealously kind, patient, self-sacrificing, merciful, loving, and wise?[13] We must be.

This is what we strive for at Avail. And everything changed for Esther when she encountered a tone and demeanor from Avail that was radically different from the ones she'd received from her pastors. She took the first abortion pill, but felt distressed. When she received an email from Avail saying simply, "Thinking of you," she replied: "Having trouble with the second pill." An Avail advocate immediately responded and provided a doctor's phone number. If she wanted to, it was not too late to try and change course. She went in and did so, and she wept as she heard her daughter's glorious heartbeat. Avail kept walking with her every step of the continuing pregnancy. Through Avail, Esther entered a community that prays for and mentors her. She is healing from her past, forgiving herself, reconnecting with her parents, and building a relationship with her child's father—who used to be the guy she resented for getting her pregnant. They are now in love and happily expectant towards the unknown.

Yes!

VICTORIOUS BUT NOT TRIUMPHALISTIC

I often tell the Avail team that the moment we stop trusting God with the mysteries of our own lives is the moment that we have nothing to say to anyone who walks through our door. No matter who we are or what we believe, we all experience the fact that life isn't what it ought to be. God's providence is hard to understand and often painful. Our lives often don't unfold as we think they should, even when we do our best, never mind when we sin. This is the common human experience, and we will sense this deep within until Jesus returns and restores the earth. We seek to walk humbly alongside our clients at Avail because we know, and remind ourselves daily, that with them we share a common human condition.

At the same time, we work with contagious joy because Christ dwells in us and advances His kingdom through us. We are not embattled defenders of a losing effort, but neither are we zealous warriors of just a righteous few. No. We are heirs of the covenant who in *meekness* will see victories won and will inherit the earth. God may allow us to encounter difficulties and sufferings that we can't comprehend, but He will also surprise us with miracles we don't expect and couldn't hope for. This is our experience of the "now but not yet" of the kingdom of God.

Tim preached almost weekly about this "now but not yet" framework of kingdom understanding, and over time it did two things for me. First, it deepened my contentment: there is no need to despair in a kingdom ruled by a righteous King. And second, it emboldened my faith: there is no need to fear in a kingdom that God has promised to advance. Instead, the kingdom of God produces in us humility, determination, and patience.

What does this mean for us as we work for the flourishing of every woman, man, and child we encounter? It means that we work victoriously but not triumphalistically. Victory is about inner confidence that God's ways will be accomplished, no matter what. Triumph, on the other hand, includes a visible display of power and the presumption of victory through a particular path. Jesus' death was victorious (and He triumphed over Satan once and for all, but unexpectedly—through crucifixion). We follow Jesus' path to victory, walking roads that include suffering; we don't walk a path of triumph that expects to win in predictable ways.

We know that abortion will not be eradicated until Jesus' return, so we do not have to be surprised by the sin we encounter. Nor do we need to be tempted to use ungodly means for godly ends. We refrain from allowing shaming or coercing measures to characterize any of our dealings, as Jesus never did. Instead, we abide in the reality that the end of any story is not up to us; we are not God. We live *confident* of the King's authority; this makes us unstoppable. And we live *submitted* to the King's authority; this makes us content.[14] We acknowledge that we can never know God's thousands of actions even within our own lives—and this keeps us from believing we understand all the details of our clients' lives. God alone changes hearts and minds, not us. Even when we think a story is over, we usually discover that it's not.

It's rare for a client to ask for me personally, since my role is not in client services. But one day, a colleague came to me saying, "Chris, a client wants to see you." I went to greet her and was confronted immediately with the tears in her eyes. She reached into her purse and pulled out a $150 check. Handing it to me, she said, "You saved my life. I just had to do something. Avail saved my life."

Mary had come to Avail for decision-making, which we offer through our Empower program. She had met with an advocate multiple times. In the end she chose abortion, as about a quarter of our clients do. But just as soon as she'd made the decision and carried it out, she found herself undone, completely devastated. In her grief and self-loathing, she returned to Avail almost immediately. For many months Mary met with an advocate in our Hope program, through which we serve women and men who have experienced abortion. The meetings changed her—so much that her friend, who had accompanied her at visits, called asking to volunteer with Avail. She was endeared to an organization that had helped her desperate friend in so many ways, though neither called themselves Christians.

So there in the hallway I stood with Mary, choked up, my eyes as tear-filled as hers. I took the check and said, "We think every woman who walks through our doors is courageous. It's a privilege to know you and receive this gift."

She smiled and turned to leave. And in her hand, I noticed a copy of C.S. Lewis' *Mere Christianity*.

Yes!

ENDURING THANKS TO TIM

Moralism—the kind that characterized me before Tim helped me see and address it—leaves little room for honesty and none for complexity. But the gospel is nothing like moralism. It frees us from every pretense and shame, and it makes space for the miraculous and hilarious. We laugh a lot at Avail. And we cry a lot at Avail. We find that reality is heartbreakingly hard. But we also find that God is good. It's not easy to sit in the paradoxes of the gospel, but that's where we have to go to follow Jesus. The Herodians and the Pharisees hated both Jesus and the gospel. One group needed to repent of sin, the other of self-righteousness, and neither would do it. But those who knew they were lost—the tax collectors, prostitutes, and sinners? They couldn't stay away from Him! And this marks our today. What an opportunity we have to follow Jesus in New York City in the twenty-first century, loving well those facing unexpected pregnancy or abortion loss! All of us are equally lost sinners in need of grace.

I live in the city and serve out of the Redeemer community because God loves New York, and I have wanted to be a small part of manifesting His great love. Tim Keller's explanation of the gospel year after year has helped me know, to the depths of my soul, that I will never outgrow the gospel or reach the end of its applications for holy living. Tim has helped me uncover my own hidden idols and the sinful patterns of my heart. And beyond that, his teaching has enabled me to see the gospel as altogether sufficient for responding to even the most intractable problems and perplexities of life, like abortion.

Christ, the Word made flesh, embodies grace and truth, and there is nothing so compelling as His beauty. In His light, we see light. It's all about Jesus. Thank you, Tim, for always living in the heart of the divine paradoxes, pointing to Jesus, and teaching me, "Yes!"

ENDNOTES

1   In his book *The Prodigal God: Recovering the Heart of the Christian Faith* (New York: Penguin Books, 2016), Tim address this idea in its entirety; he directly speaks about two ways to be your own Savior and Lord (50–51).

2   "We can do no great things, only small things with great love." This quote is a paraphrased version or personal interpretation of a statement made by Mother Teresa (www.motherteresa.org/08_info/Quotesf.html) which was the inspiration for the quote "Grace bids me to do little things with great love and forbids me to do great things with little love."

3   In 1 John 4:19–21, the apostle John appeals to conscience and logic when he argues from the greater to the lesser. No one can claim to love God (whom one has not seen), if one does not love his brother, whom one has seen. John has a harsh name for that person: liar. The clear point is that it's harder to love what is not seen than what is seen. If we do not love well the woman and man in front of our very eyes, we must realize we are hypocrites asking the man and woman unexpectedly pregnant to do what we ourselves are not doing.

4   Timothy Keller, "The Gospel-Shaped Life" (sermon), *The Gospel Coalition,* December 28, 2019, https://www.youtube.com/watch?v=-mu_CLg2Nfo.

5   Timothy Keller (@timkellernyc), "The gospel says you are more sinful and flawed than you ever dared believe, but more accepted and loved than you ever dared hope," Twitter, October 30, 2018,

    https://twitter.com/timkellernyc/status/1057203962934452224.

6   These theological truths are demonstrated in numerous scriptural references including: John 3:16;
     Titus 2:13; 1 John 4:2; Rom. 3:23; 1 Cor. 1:2; Eph. 2:19; Gen. 1:26; James 3:9; Rom. 1:18–25; Matt. 3:2;
     Matt. 16:19; Matt. 19:14; Rev. 11:15; Dan. 7:13–14; Rom. 3:23; Rom. 6:23; James 1:15; Matt. 20:16; Mic.
     6:8; John 12:24.

7   A Hebrew word that is derived from a root that denotes "wholeness" or "completeness" and is often
     translated "peace."

8   This paradox of loving someone unconditionally who is intentionally choosing to do something that
     harms you is most clearly evidenced in Luke 23:34. As the Roman soldiers nail Jesus to the cross, He
     prays, "Father, forgive them, for they know not what they do." At this moment, the soldiers are in the
     process of executing Jesus. And yet, instead of condemning them, He prays a prayer that springs from
     a heart of unconditional love for them and is manifested in the very action of being nailed to a cross.

9   Eph. 2:8–9; Matt. 23:23; Rom. 3:23; James 2:10; Matt. 5:17; Matt. 12:24–26.

10   An example of this type of cultural assumption can be found in John 9:2 when the disciples turn to
     Jesus to ask, "Who sinned, this man or his parents, that he was born blind?"

11   In his book *The Prodigal God: Recovering the Heart of the Christian Faith* (New York, NY: Penguin Books,
     2016), Tim writes, "All life-changing love is some kind of substitutionary sacrifice" (61).

12   Lifeway Research, "Study of Women who have had an Abortion and Their Views on Church,"
     2015, http://www.lifewayresearch.com/wp-content/uploads/2015/11/Care-Net-Final-
     Quantitative-Report.pdf.

13   Ibid.

14   This idea was shaped by the following tweet from Tim: "Think of fanatical people. They're overbear-
     ing, insensitive, and harsh. Why? It's not because they are too Christian but because they are not
     Christian enough. They are fanatically zealous, but they are not fanatically humble, sensitive, empa-
     thetic, or forgiving—as Christ was." Timothy Keller (@timkellernyc), Twitter, May 23, 2021, https://
     twitter.com/timkellernyc/status/1396503762005540866?lang=en.

15   In their introduction to *Uncommon Ground: Living Faithfully in a World of Difference* (Nashville, TN:
     Nelson Books, 2020), authors Timothy Keller and John Inazu write, "It is with that posture we offer
     this book: a call to engage the world as we find it, doing so with confident hope rather than stifling
     anxiety" (xxi).

MIKE **BONTRAGER**

Business

THE BURNING BUSH

When I look back over the past thirty years, Tim Keller stands out as the person who most shaped—or should I say reshaped—my view of God, the world, and my place in it. Not only did he synthesize and communicate the gospel in a way that made sense to me at a time when Christianity was fading as an influence on my life, but this spiritual transformation dramatically affected the financial company I founded as well as the network of organizations I now lead. While Tim would not claim to have expertise in business or finance, his influence was one of the most critical forces behind the success of my growing firm. And watching Tim inspire a powerful movement across the global church led me to envision my numerous entrepreneurial ventures as vehicles for creating and driving societal movements.

Growing up, I had all the blessings of a loving home, caring and attentive parents, and a church community that loved and cared for each other. My father was a conservative Mennonite minister, which meant that we were at church anytime the doors were open. Worldly influences were either forbidden or minimized. We were the good people; most outside of our faith community were considered either bad, misguided, or naïve. My concept of evangelism was to move people to the good side. While I was taught the concept of salvation through grace—the idea that it was God's unmerited favor that made me justified before God—it was drowned out by an emphasis on personal piety and having the right theology. I set out to uphold these inherited ideals and become the young man I believed God was calling me to be.

After graduating from a Christian college—my entire education to this point had been in Christian schools—I landed a job on Wall Street. After marrying my high school sweetheart, we essentially bifurcated our lives such that we became active in our local church and worked to remain moral in our jobs, but largely left engagement on spiritual matters to Sundays.

Wanting to follow Christ's command to share my faith, I sought opportunities to engage non-believers in faith conversations. But for the first time I encountered people whose thoughtful arguments and perspectives dismantled the strawman arguments I had been taught on why non-believers did not believe in God. In fact, over time I was alarmed to find myself agreeing more with their arguments explaining why they weren't Christians than with my own arguments for why they should be. The dissonance between the way I learned to interpret the Bible and what I saw happening in the world began to grow more acute. I came reluctantly to realize that I no longer believed, and I needed to decide whether to maintain a Christian front, or whether I should reveal myself as an unbeliever and deal with all the family and social fallout that would follow.

I revealed my dilemma to my long-time friend and college roommate. He didn't preach or try to dissuade me but simply entered into the significant emotions that attended the moment. He gave me a cassette tape (it was 1994) of a little-known pastor in New York named Tim Keller and asked me to listen. When I got home, I listened, then listened again, then a third time, and then subscribed to the series. Tim preached on passages I knew well—many I had memorized—but I heard a very different message in each one. When I received his classic sermons on Luke 15, the "parable of the prodigal son"— which would become his book *The Prodigal God*—I was shocked and moved. The key point of the book is that there are two ways of running from God: the obvious way reflected by the younger "prodigal son" who pursued worldly pleasures, or the non-obvious way reflected by the older son who played by his father's rules to earn spiritual credits. The concept that *my own righteousness could keep me from God* was radical for me. When Tim talked about "elder brother lostness" I realized that he was talking about me. I was the one approaching God transactionally—keeping my nose clean in exchange for God's approval. But as I began to understand God's grace and the relationship He desired with me, my entire understanding of God, the Bible, and the church began to change.

I would eagerly await the latest cassette tape and listen to each sermon two or three times. During this time, the Bible almost felt like a new book because I was reading it with a deeper understanding of my need for grace. Biblical stories that I knew well took on new or completely different meanings. My appetite for spiritual nourishment and prayer exploded, and for several years God invaded my life in ways that I had never before experienced. For the first time the overarching story of the Bible began to make sense. It felt so much more cohesive and consistent than the paradigm that I had been operating from.

I'm aware (and delighted!) that my story to this point is a common one. Tim's preaching has profoundly illuminated the gospel for tens of thousands, possibly hundreds of thousands, of elder brothers like me. While Tim's teaching was essential in reorienting my understanding of my need for God's grace, his impact went much further. The less common part reflected in my story is that I had the privilege of starting and growing a company where I could put my understanding of God's purposes into organizational practice. Both the holistic vision Tim offered of God's purposes in the world and his methods for nurturing a movement around vision dramatically influenced my entrepreneurial vision.

BUSINESS AS A BURNING BUSH

Several years earlier I had left my job on Wall Street and started a financial derivatives advisory firm. We moved to Pennsylvania with our young kids to be near family and start the company. In those early days, a greater purpose for the company did not even cross my mind. While I might have prayed for the business from time to time, my hopes were primarily focused on financial success.

Several years into starting the business, my spiritual transformation began. I looked for resources to understand how to build a business consistent with this powerful new understanding of grace I learned from the dozens of Tim's sermons I had so voraciously consumed. I met with Christian entrepreneurs and business leaders to hear how they were integrating their faith into their ventures. Most of what I heard boiled down to two models: your company as a platform to share your faith, or your company as a tool to fund Christian causes. While both are of some value, I felt called to something more. Tim's preaching on God's intentions for a new heaven and a new earth—and our calling to be *restorers of a creation in disrepair*—led me to believe that God wanted to use my company to create *shalom* (a holistic form of well-being) in my little corner of a broken world, rather than simply as a vehicle to fund Christian causes or as an evangelistic platform. I started pondering how my company could provide a taste of the restoration God ultimately intends to bring into being.

In one sermon that was particularly meaningful to me, Tim preached on Moses and the burning bush. In this story, God reveals His intention for the Hebrew people and for Moses by attracting him to a bush in the wilderness that was in flames. What is a burning bush? Tim explained it as something totally natural doing something supernatural. It caught Moses' eye. It drew him in. He went across a ravine to see it. Tim suggested that this is a metaphor for the life of a Christian in an unbelieving world. I remember thinking, "I want to build a burning bush company. On the outside, it would look like a typical company. But people would sense that there was something supernatural going on such that people would be drawn to it, whether or not they were believers."

This burning bush idea shaped how I and my colleagues (who had a range of spiritual beliefs) built our company. Starting with our purpose for existence and extending to everything, from how we treated people, to the way we owned our mistakes, to how we valued client and employee trust over profit, our culture and ethos was radically different from most Wall Street firms, especially in the nineties. One self-described secular employee, who joined our company largely because he was attracted to our culture, once challenged me that we were secretly a religious company because he saw how my faith was working its way into decisions. I countered that we were values-based, rather than faith-based. While my values originate from my faith, I recognize that people could share my values without sharing my faith. This employee attempted to persuade me that since faith wasn't the prerequisite for gaining influence within our organization, it should not be viewed as important. That discussion afforded the opportunity to explain how my spiritual transformation radically changed how I thought about building a company. I told him that my guess was that, had God not radically altered my spiritual trajectory (i.e., through the preaching of Tim Keller), he would not have found our company so attractive. It was the burning bush that he was drawn to.

During my tenure at the company, I regularly held sessions with all newer employees during which we went over what our company stood for, the standards we expected, and the external and internal character qualities essential to our success—things like integrity, humility, and trust. After leading a session in one of our foreign offices, I was approached by a young man who asked, "Where did this come from?" A bit surprised, I asked what he meant. He replied that he had worked for several financial firms and the elevation of these concepts was so different from anything he had experienced. We ended up in a lengthy discussion about how God had transformed my life and how it had deeply affected how I endeavored to build the culture. He too had grown up in a strict religious family with little understanding of grace, so my story resonated with him. I pointed him to several of Tim's sermons, which he eagerly sought out. He was attracted to the burning bush.

In the late nineties I began attending Redeemer Presbyterian's annual multi-day forum called the Entrepreneurship Initiative. I was thrilled to meet so many people thinking about their companies as restorers in a world marked by brokenness. Tim's introductory comments focused on how the creative process of the entrepreneur reflects the character of God, the author of creation. This annual event shaped my view of entrepreneurship and connected me with a community of entrepreneurs seeking to apply these redemptive ideas in our businesses. Without the influence of Tim and the initiatives he started, I doubt if I would have seen my financial derivatives business as a vehicle for restoration in a world marked by brokenness.

OBSERVING A MOVEMENT IN ACTION

As I became more closely connected to Tim's work and witnessed his methods, I learned still new lessons about how to pursue broader societal change beyond a single organization.

The idea that there is an extremely wide and growing gap in trust between Wall Street and Main Street is not controversial. Our company's mission eventually became "to catalyze and model the restoration of trust in the capital markets." We were a relatively small player in finance but in the niche markets that we served, our dedication to trust maximizing rather than profit maximizing served to establish us as the go-to player worldwide. We were able to attract incredibly talented and principled employees and an uncommonly loyal client base. And within our niche, we were able to accumulate significant influence. At the same time, we were a small part of the vast financial system and it was clear that broader change in our markets needed to be a collaborative undertaking—we couldn't do it alone.

Our company called our attempt to catalyze trust in the capital market our "Quest"—an audacious goal toward which we strived but that would never fully be realized. For us to advance in our quest, we needed to catalyze a movement, a paradigm shift in the way entrepreneurs and business leaders thought about their roles in financial markets. As we began strategizing on how to identify and approach like-minded financial firms who could partner with us on this quest, I reflected on how Tim, Redeemer Presbyterian Church, and Redeemer City to City had within a generation changed a paradigm of how many Christians all around the world think about the gospel, their vocation, and their interaction with culture.

Many charismatic and articulate leaders have created large followings; however, very few succeed in changing how a generation thinks. I remember meeting with Tim and his capable team in the mid-2000s as they were strategizing the launch of Redeemer City to City and hearing their vision of creating a global gospel movement by, as I remember it, launching or assisting in the launch of ten thousand new churches in cities in the next twenty-five years. While I was impressed with the ambitiousness of the vision, it struck me as improbable in a world that was increasingly hostile to Christianity. But we are now in a position to appraise the impact of the first stage of this work and conclude that, surely with God's blessing and the integral collaboration of likeminded believers and unaffiliated organizations, a vital, worldwide gospel movement has been brought into being.

The methods Tim employed were essential to this movement and were inspiring to me as I endeavored to cultivate a restorative movement within finance. Indeed, I believe his methods serve as a tremendous sociological and organizational model for creating and sustaining a movement dynamic. He has done this not only through his books and teaching material, but also through the thousands of pastors and church leaders he has mentored either directly or through organizations he started. It is thus likely that Tim's enduring legacy will be a movement that went far beyond him. Many people who have never heard of Tim Keller will have been shaped by the gospel movement that he played a significant role in shepherding.

I have come to see that Tim brought together three elements necessary for a paradigm-shifting movement—skillfully articulated ideas, examples of those ideas in action, and a community of practice. Many leaders and organizations are successful in one or two of these areas but only a few have combined all three elements in the right way. When working together, with each element introduced at the right time, they create a flywheel effect which continues to strengthen each element and advances the movement.

First, paradigm-shifting movements need paradigm-shifting ideas and content communicated in an accessible way. Skillful communicators with paradigm-shifting content often end up as regulars on the conference circuit. The temptation for those with this capability is to cultivate their personal brand and enjoy their celebrity status. When this happens, their impact tends to be stronger on their direct followers than on a movement that will outlive them. Tim clearly has resisted the temptation toward celebrity status. He did not start publishing until long after Redeemer gained organizational maturity—and only then because it was a critical part of a church planting strategy. He resisted taking speaking engagements unless it fit into a strategic plan of advancing the movement. He has used his popularity as a tool to serve the greater mission of advancing the movement, rather than advancing his personal brand.

Secondly, paradigm-shifting movements need to be nurtured through successful examples of these ideas and content in action. When ideas are different and new, it is unclear whether they can survive in a real-world environment. I have watched Tim's patience as he built Redeemer Presbyterian slowly over the years and resisted the temptation to speak widely and write about what he had learned while building the church. When ready, he did not simply communicate what he had learned. Instead, he launched Redeemer City to City to help enterprising pastors imagine and launch churches that might look very different from Redeemer, while sharing the same theological mission and vision. By focusing on core principles (often summarized under the headings Gospel, City, and Movement) he left room for church planters around the world to contextualize them into their specific situations. As a result, the movement now encompasses like-minded churches in many different contexts, cultures, and Christian traditions, increasing the strength of the movement. The fact that City to City has helped to launch far more non-Presbyterian churches than Presbyterian churches points to Tim's interest in creating a movement and not simply an organization.

Last, paradigm-shifting movements need to build a community around the ideas and content which serves to incubate, mentor, and fund those who are on the front lines of putting the ideas into practice. This is a community where like-minded individuals can create sounding boards, and can inspire, challenge, and learn from each other. Such communities nurture friendship and camaraderie, the strength of which further advances the movement. Tim and his team have planted a small community that grew up around the initial content and ideas behind Redeemer Presbyterian into a global community of Christ-followers who are incubating new churches and initiatives, further strengthening the movement far past what one individual or organization could sustain.

APPLYING THE MOVEMENT PARADIGM IN MY DOMAIN

This movement has heavily shaped how this generation of Christians view the gospel, how we are called to interact with the world, and the importance of our vocations in joining God in the renewal of all things—whether in finance, medicine, education, or any other realm. Indeed, watching and learning from Tim's leadership of a gospel movement has deeply influenced how I think about the importance of movements in my own organizational contexts.

In the years before my retirement from the financial firm I founded, we sought to emulate the strategy Tim used to further our quest to restore trust to the capital markets. We began by working with a research firm to study the nascent philosophies of various groups that understood the disrepair of the financial system and were creating alternative models. For over twenty-five years we had wrestled, largely alone, with building an alternative to a traditional financial firm, and we had learned through success and failure. But now we joined convenings of like-minded entrepreneurs to share learnings, encourage each other, and further strengthen this budding movement as well as our resolve. This movement is still small, and it remains to be seen whether it will be able to make a meaningful impact on the dysfunctions embedded within capitalism.

After twenty-eight years of building the financial firm I founded, I retired and poured my attention into an entrepreneurial and movement-oriented approach to seeking shalom within our local community. Our ambition is to encourage our community to think about thriving in a holistic and comprehensive way. Our organization is a collection of for-profit and non-profit ventures and projects that we have either started or partnered with others to start, building an ecosystem in which everyone, regardless of their background, race, or socioeconomic status, has the ability to thrive. With initiatives as varied as a community beer garden, an accessible fourteen-mile nature trail loop, a project memorializing our community's unsung but vital role in the Underground Railroad, and a backbone organization supporting all community organizations focused on reducing poverty, we are seeking to weave the fabric of our community more tightly, to allow everyone to enjoy the beauty of our area and to benefit from its increasing economic prosperity.

This holistic approach to community development is counter to the traditional method where organizations tend to be siloed, each targeting a specific aspect of community life. There is a growing network of communities around the country taking this holistic approach, experimenting with different ideas, sharing their findings, and encouraging each other. We have had the good fortune of networking with many of these like-minded entrepreneurs, cultivating friendships and exchanging ideas. While this growing movement toward holistic community development is not Christian in name, we have found that many of the leaders who are part of this informal network are motivated by God's call to love their communities and, I suspect, many would cite Tim's teachings about the gospel and the city as informing their vision and motivating their action. His influence permeates these discussions.

Around the 2020 election I was in conversation with some other concerned Christian leaders wrestling with the question of whether the term "evangelical" has become so politicized that it no longer serves as a useful label to describe our faith or practice. My reshaped view of the gospel often makes me wince when the media references evangelicals and how they are engaging the world. When I reflect on my discomfort with how this term has been distorted, I realize that, had God not transformed my life and career through Tim's ministry, most likely I would neatly fit into one of the polarized camps fomenting division in our country. I would probably have built an ethically profit-maximizing company rather than one that sought to challenge the disrepair in our industry. I doubt that my "retirement" would be spent seeking the shalom of the community where God has placed us.

But Tim, through his preaching and the organizations he built, has pointed to a third way—the Jesus way—the way of seeing ourselves as more deeply flawed than we are ready to admit and more deeply loved than we could ever dare hope. It is a way of seeing our vocations and ventures as redemptive, as vehicles through which we can join God in the renewal of all things. It is this understanding of grace that provides the supernatural resources to see others through the eyes of God, to love them as precious and valuable, regardless of who they are, what they believe, or what they do. This is the burning bush that points to the one who can heal a broken world.

JUDY **CHA**

Counseling

TEARING DOWN THE IDOLS

Tim's incredible gift of communicating the gospel in simple yet profound ways is acknowledged all around the globe. Through his teaching, he ingrained one consistent theme in my heart—the gospel, God's story of grace, changes everything! As Tim so skillfully conveyed this message, the gospel has indeed changed me and is still changing my heart—my identity, my relationships, my purpose and meaning in life. I imagine there are countless stories of changed lives as God used Tim to convey His truth. However, people may not be aware of how much Tim's ministry helped strengthen the relevance of Christian Counseling.

In this tribute to Tim, I will share how his writings and teachings have influenced both my personal thinking about counseling, as well as the way Redeemer Counseling Services (RCS) approaches counseling. Then, I will share how his vision for the gospel movement expanded our counseling ministry into a resource for the whole city and beyond. Finally, I will share how his challenge to engage in cultural renewal has led Redeemer Counseling Services to participate in research with the desire to make gospel perspectives applicable in the therapeutic process.

CONTRIBUTION TO CHRISTIAN COUNSELING:

During Tim's early years as the senior pastor, Redeemer Counseling Services, a counseling ministry within Redeemer Presbyterian Church, was established as an extension of pastoral care. By establishing a counseling ministry, Redeemer acknowledged that counseling is an integral part of pastoral ministry and validated the role of counselors in the work of helping people personalize the gospel. Tim affirmed that we cannot differentiate between "spiritual problems" (that supposedly pastors alone deal with) and psychological problems (that supposedly counselors deal with), since there is no biblical reason to suppose that the spirit and the psyche are two different things. However, Tim recognized that there is a need for concentrated training and experience in counseling, because he views counseling issues to be extremely complex. So when New York state regulations required a waiver from the state in 2009 to hire licensed counselors to work at Redeemer Church, the leadership sought legal assistance to make sure licensed professionals could provide care at RCS. To date, Redeemer Presbyterian Church is the only religious entity that houses a counseling ministry that offers professional counseling provided by licensed counselors.

Moreover, Redeemer Presbyterian Church is the only church in New York City to provide training for Continuing Education Units to other licensed counselors. I believe this was possible because of Tim's appreciation for specialized training and his acknowledgement that the issues that brought people to seek counseling—like depression/anxiety, addictions, infidelity, and abuse—have multiple root causes and varied symptoms that require a great deal of experience and time to understand and therefore to treat. Tim recognized that most pastors lack counseling training, just as most counselors lack sufficient training in spirituality and theology. Thus, a church that insists that pastors do all the counseling simply will not offer their people the best possible pastoral care. Tim had the mindset that a counseling ministry would help steward the time of the pastors and elders so that they could give themselves more equitably to the whole flock and entrust the complex, more personal work of healing and change to the counselors.

Having this in mind, I understood that RCS is an extension of pastoral care, and that ultimately, the context for soul care cannot be limited to one-on-one counseling relationships, but must involve the whole Christian community. Certainly, heart change initiated in the counseling relationship should have a ripple effect in all other relational circles, including the Christian community. At the same time, every Christian community should foster heart change in people who are part of that community. This interdependence between the individual and the body of Christ shaped the way we practice counseling at RCS.

Firstly, we assess prospective clients' spirituality, such as whether they believe in God, attend a church, and how much influence their faith has in their daily lives. Knowing where people are in their faith journeys helps us determine how the gospel can be relevant in the process of counseling. Moreover, one of our treatment goals is to help people engage in the bigger community of believers if they are not yet integrated in the body of the church.

Secondly, our counselors collaborate with other care providers, including pastors and ministry leaders, when caring for people, (with proper consents, of course). RCS counselors also participate in weekly group supervision, presenting cases and seeking input from one another, because we recognize our shortcomings as individuals who need input from the bigger community of colleagues. We know there is tremendous value in seeking wisdom when helping those under our care.

Finally, we apply the interdependence between the individual and the church body in our process of hiring counselors, which includes a screening for theological alignment and faith practices as well as clinical expertise. Every newly hired counselor goes through a training period regardless of their educational background and clinical experience to learn how to apply the RCS approach in their counseling.

CONTRIBUTION TO RCS COUNSELING APPROACH

Tim advocated for diversity among the counseling staff. Since counseling is an extension of pastoral care, the counseling staff should be reflective of the whole urban Christian community. As such, RCS was and still is staffed with a mixture of both seminary trained biblical counselors and clinically trained licensed professionals. Although the staff is united in love for Christ and in our desire for the gospel to be relevant in the practice of counseling, we come from diverse cultures, ethnicities, and training backgrounds. Ideally, a primary benefit of a diverse staff is the learning that stems from it, but the process of learning from one another has not always been pleasant or easy.

Tim is a master at presenting his point of view without offending others who hold a different view, which may explain his fondness for discourse. In any case, I do believe there is collective wisdom in diversity; a lack of diversity could cause our knowledge and experience to stagnate. Given the diversity of our staff, our conversations naturally flowed to the question of integration between theology and psychology. We believe that God gives us knowledge of what is wrong in the human psyche and heart not only through "special revelation" of the Bible but also through the "general revelation" of human empirical observation. However, our concern was how to apply this in practice.

Tim's analysis of the four views on the relationship between psychology and Christianity defined the boundaries of integration practiced at RCS.[1] His summary and analysis of the four views have been widely read among Christians counselors and ministry leaders. For RCS, it became a guide in developing a common framework for all staff to apply in the practice of counseling. Almost two decades ago, a team of our counselors devoted to Christ and their profession began working on a framework for therapy that prioritizes the gospel while being informed by the truths in psychology. The foundation of our theory is that personal identity can and should be derived from God, as we are beings made in His image.

Personally, being raised in a Christian home, I believed in Christ as a young child. However, I did not fully understand the implications of God's amazing grace in forming my identity until I came to Redeemer more than twenty-four years ago. One key implication of the gospel that significantly changed how I viewed myself and that shaped my lens as a counselor was the realization that my identity is *received, not earned*. Although I believed in Christ's substitutionary atonement and that neither my goodness nor my badness defines who I am, for most of my early years as a Christian, I lived as one seeking to be good enough to "earn" my place as His child. Even now, as an older Christian, though I am more aware of my tendencies, I still—often unconsciously—engage in this quest to pursue my way of self-redemption to justify myself, utilizing various strategies to deem myself worthy, acceptable, and good. My propensity to construct my own system of self-redemption, or the idol of self, was further explained through Tim's book *Counterfeit Gods* which became foundational in raising my self-awareness and shaping the Gospel-Centered Integrative Framework for Therapy (GIFT)—the RCS approach to counseling.

In the GIFT, we recognize that the core problem of humanity is our tendency to rely on ourselves to create our own system of self-redemption. We use various strategies and/or idols to try to justify ourselves, cover up our shame, and assert an identity that is worthy and acceptable. In *Counterfeit Gods*, Tim suggests that any despair we experience ultimately results from the adoption of idols, such as money, success, relationships, and power. These idols are objects, persons, or pursuits that we use to feel okay about ourselves. When we pursue these idols, we worship "counterfeit gods" by placing our trust in objects and pursuits that provide us with a sense of self-worth, as opposed to receiving this through an intimate relationship with God. These counterfeit gods can be so central in our lives that if we were to lose them, we may feel as if our lives would not be worth living. Tim wisely points out that our idols are often good things that become our ultimate things as a result of our misplaced affection for them—the affection that should be given to God. So anything we pursue can become idolatrous when our desire for it becomes inordinate. This nuanced perspective highlighted that the objects, people, and pursuits were not necessarily bad in themselves, but that the problem is our hearts' misplaced affections—loving something more than God.

Tim's version of how idolatry works clarified further the complexity of idol formation as well as the complexity of relinquishing it. Reading his book, *Walking with God in Pain and Suffering* confirmed for me that our experiences of pain are closely associated with our idolatry—that another function of idolatry is to suppress the pain of what we experience here, which ultimately reinforces the pain of our shame as a result of losing our connection with God, the Creator from whom we are to derive our identity. Unfortunately, every idol fails to fully suppress our pain, which leads us to greater distress and despair. However, recognizing this association between our idols and our pain allows people to empathize with rather than revile/reject their fallen state and more readily turn to God for His healing—thus, they can experience progressively more freedom from their idolatry.

I grew up with the notion that strong Christians should not be affected by suffering and pain. But the truth is that good Christians should rejoice in suffering. However, Tim does not minimize our experience of pain and urges us to recognize our suffering and its corresponding emotions. He gives validity to our reactive emotions to pain; rather than suppressing them, he encourages us to grieve, to pour out our souls to God and receive His comfort. With this understanding, the GIFT recognizes the hardship of relinquishing idols and that, in part, is connected to our efforts to suppress our pain and avoid the shame that is so deeply ingrained in us as a result of innate sin nature. So, helping people identify past wounds and appropriately grieve their pain are critical aspects of our counseling approach. It is in this phase that people become more willing to engage with God.

Of course, the aspect of Tim's teaching that was most influential in the shaping of the GIFT was his emphasis on the centrality of the gospel in changing and healing hearts. When the gospel becomes progressively internalized and our relationship with Christ becomes more personal, we increasingly turn away from our systems of self-redemption and turn toward God, relying on His grace alone to justify us. Internalizing the gospel leads us more and more to relinquish our systems of self-redemption and experience the Spirit leading our lives.

For most of my life, I knew in my head that the gospel justified me— what Jesus did on the cross covers my shame and frees me from the striving to feel okay about myself. But the shift in my faith journey happened when this knowledge became a lived experience for me. Under Tim's shepherding,

I learned that the gospel is not only something to be understood, but to be experienced in relationship with the Living God—that doctrinal knowledge must become experiential knowledge. In the GIFT, our aim is to facilitate experiential encounters with God in which people can experience Him as someone who identifies with their pain and empathizes with them. Helping people approach God with more honesty and vulnerability, and guiding them them as they learn to express their deepest anguish directly to God is critical to heart change, because this honest, wrestling process with God is the beginning of personalizing the gospel and engaging in a new, deeper relational interaction with Him.

Another key principle in the GIFT learned from Tim is the concept of contextualized care. The term "contextualized" is from his book *Center Church*. I understood that in order to facilitate a process in which the truth of the gospel is deeply personalized and becomes relevant to people, counseling must be contextualized to each person. This idea of contextualization became the heart of the entire counseling process and the most essential principle in the GIFT. It is defined as giving the care that people need in the way it will be best received. We believe that counseling cannot be the same for every person or every issue. Given a person's unique set of dispositions, experiences, subjective interpretations, and spiritual receptivity and maturity, counseling should be specific to each person and their story and struggles. When we contextualize skillfully, people become more open to the direction of the counseling process and to receiving the care they need. Contextualization allows the counseling process to be personally meaningful and effective to a diverse group of people—even those who do not share our beliefs about God.

The GIFT is the common ground that we share as RCS staff. Our shared view about integration, our understanding of the real problem of humanity, and the solution in the gospel are what unify us. It has been my experience that the strength of what we have in common allows us to exchange healthy dialogue to learn from and appreciate our diverse training backgrounds and perspectives. I imagine this is what Tim was aiming for when he advocated for diversity among our staff.

CONTRIBUTION TO THE CITY AND BEYOND

Tim's teaching influenced our counseling approach at Redeemer Counseling Services. But his vision for the gospel movement and for a church that is not for itself but for the city also led RCS to become was it is today. When I arrived at RCS in 1998, we were a full-time staff of three with another three to four very part-time counselors. At that time, those who sought counseling at RCS were predominantly from Redeemer Church. After 9/11, however, Redeemer Church became the hub of the city for pastoral care. Since then, RCS has become a resource providing Gospel-Centered Professional Counseling for the tristate area. Today, RCS is staffed with more than fifty people providing over five hundred counseling sessions each week, and caring for approximately two thousand people annually. Even though the COVID-19 pandemic shut down everything in the spring of 2020, we were able to stay connected digitally and did not stopped caring for people during this time of high distress. I've never been so grateful for the Internet!

Even before the pandemic, we were facing a mental health crisis—a growing number of people were seeking counseling care. In fact, the Department of Health & Human Services has projected that we will have a shortage of mental health providers to address this growing need by 2025. In 2018, in anticipation of this need, RCS expanded its reach and launched the equipping arm to train ministry leaders and professional counselors to counsel utilizing the GIFT. I know the need for counseling has exponentially increased during the pandemic. Although I cannot fully imagine what the impact will be, I do expect that there will be a long-term fallout from the pandemic on our mental health.

Since the pandemic began, RCS has not only continued to provide over 23,000 sessions virtually, but in addition, churches, ministries, and organizations reached out to RCS to help care for their congregations, staff, and constituents. We received over sixty requests in 2020 to run workshops, trainings, and process groups. Then, in early 2021, we launched our first written curriculum, *Mourning with Hope,* to help churches and ministries run grief groups, forecasting the need of many who have suffered losses during this pandemic.

The advancements in technology have enabled us to not only continue to meet people's mental health needs, but to also realize that our vision for reaching people with the redemptive power of the gospel will progressively expand. Already in 2020, our fellows program was able to reach beyond the tristate area, virtually training pastors and ministry leaders from other parts of the country. I'd never imagined that RCS would become as wide reaching as we are currently, but now, I can foresee the gospel movement, sharing the importance of gospel-centered counseling care, continuing through virtual platforms.

CONTRIBUTION TO CULTURAL RENEWAL

Tim's keen awareness of the shifts in our culture taught me to be mindful of how our culture is shaping our views on mental health and counseling care. According to a Barna survey in February of 2018, the stigma around counseling is decreasing. The majority of the population believe that mental health is a legitimate concern, and more people are open to not only talking about mental health, but to seeking care, especially among the younger generation (teens to young adults).

More than a decade ago, I read an article written by Paul Bloom, a professor of psychology at Yale. One statement captured my attention and has intrigued me ever since. He wrote, "The great conflict between science and religion in the last century was over evolutionary biology. In this century, it will be over psychology, and the stakes are nothing less than our souls."[2] Tim raised my awareness that as a society, we are becoming more and more individualistic, searching for an identity narrative that redeems our internalized shame. I suspect this evolution in our culture will cause more people to seek counseling, not only because people will feel more isolated in their struggle as a result of individualism, but because counseling is becoming more than a context for treating symptoms and resolving conflicts. Counseling is becoming a context in which we wrestle with the existential questions of identity and meaning in life. So, all the more, I feel the urgency to make the gospel relevant in the arena of counseling, because mental health should not be separated from our spiritual health.

Consistent with his commitment for cultural renewal, Tim's teaching on the intersection between our faith and work regularly challenged me to engage with the field of psychology. Having been a Christian counselor for more than two decades and sensing that Christian counseling is perceived as somehow subpar to mainstream mental health care, it became important to me that Christian counseling as a whole gain credibility in the field. At the same time, in the last twenty-plus years, there was a major shift toward religion and spirituality in the field, in which scholars began acknowledging our spiritual nature and accepting spirituality in psychology as a new interdisciplinary blend. From my perspective, this shift gave legitimacy to integrating faith beliefs and practices into psychotherapy and to analyze this integration. As such, I saw this as an opportunity to engage the field through research—to offer our gospel-centered perspectives as another possible way of alleviating our mental health struggles.

Since 2012, RCS has participated in research and completed four projects, resulting in publications in professional journals and presentations at the national American Psychological Association (APA) convention. The most recent study was funded by the John Templeton Foundation, which was conducted in partnership with Fordham University. The research team included Tim as the expert on theology, Dr. Elena Kim as the psychotherapy researcher, and myself as the clinical expert. The goal of the project was to identify and detail the mechanisms of heart change or, as we call it at RCS, the process of repentance and faith. All of these studies have provided support that the GIFT may be linked to favorable outcomes. Dr. Elena Kim, Tim and I will be authoring a chapter in an APA published textbook titled *Handbook of Spiritually-Integrated Psychotherapies*. This will be the first publication that introduces RCS's Gospel-Centered Integrative Framework for Therapy. With the desire to provide effective gospel-centered treatments, we will continue our research even further.

In closing, it is undeniable that Tim has had a tremendous influence in shaping our counseling approach, our reach as a counseling ministry, and how we engage the field through research. However, I cannot end this tribute without recognizing Kathy and her profound contributions to RCS. Having studied counseling herself, she has always provided support for not only the counseling ministry, but also for me as another woman serving the church. I have consulted her for theological soundness when defining our approach and her feedback has helped us clarify our perspectives. She has also been the chief editor for our written materials for years, including the documentation of the GIFT, which we use to train all of our newly hired counselors as well as our fellows. Over the years, I have appreciated the Kellers' encouragement and support and their trust in me as the Director of Counseling. I came to Redeemer disillusioned by ministry, confused about God's calling for my life. God has truly used Tim and Kathy's ministry to change me and shape the ministry that I am a part of now. I have been immensely blessed to have known Tim and Kathy. Without a doubt, it has been a real privilege to be a recipient of their ministry at Redeemer.

ENDNOTES

1   Dr. Timothy Keller, "Four Models of Counseling," *Redeemer City to City,* https://c4265878.ssl.cf2.
     rackcdn.com/redeemer.1709191425.Four_Models_of_Counseling_in_Pastoral_Ministry.pdf.
2   Paul Bloom, "The Duel Between Body and Soul," *New York Times,* September 10, 2004, https://www.
     nytimes.com/2004/09/10/opinion/the-duel-between-body-and-soul.html.

BILL **KURTZ**

Leadership

A FRAMEWORK FOR FAITH IN THE WORKPLACE

The last bars of the doxology drift from the roll-out organ as Tim Keller walks to the front of the Hunter College auditorium stage, sermon notes in hand. I remember the sense of joy and anticipation in the room. God was working in Redeemer Presbyterian Church. We all felt it. The Holy Spirit was alive in this unlikely gathering of believers, seekers, and non-believers in New York City in the early 1990s. As Tim used to say, people came to New York to make a career, to earn big bucks on Wall Street, or to make it on Broadway. They did not come to find Jesus.

And yet, many of us did find Jesus, as well as a new way to think about our lives in His image, not the image of New York City. Tim's teaching did not take us out of the city or out of our vocations, but rather helped us lean into the city, and to approach our vocations with a kingdom frame. Tim wove the gospel into our ambitious work dreams, the pulsing energy of the city streets, and the fabric of our communities. Through the gospel brought to life at Redeemer, we conceived of a new way of understanding the world and our vocations.

And for me, Tim's patient teaching and intellect has been a catalyst. As a young Wall Street investment banker, I asked the question, how do I believe in God? Does faith magically emerge in my mind, my heart, both? Under Tim's teaching, I learned to feel, to understand what faith really is. Through Redeemer, God pursued me and I found God. I experienced the integration of thought into faith, normalizing the idea that Christian faith can be intellectual and mysterious at the same time. I left so many of Tim's teachings with so much to think about.

In my early Christian journey, his teaching wove the disparate parts of my life—faith, family, work, and community—into a new Kingdom vision. I began my career just after college as an investment banker at the Chase

Manhatten Bank. In so many ways, I was Redeemer's target audience. I read about Redeemer in a *Wall Street Journal* article and decided to check it out. As I grappled with the "climb the career ladder at all costs" mentality of New York, Tim preached a gospel that helped me see vocation as a part of a larger and more complete whole. I eventually felt called to pursue a different vocation where I could directly serve the city, so I left Chase to begin working as an assistant principal, teacher, and coach at Catholic K–8 School in the South Bronx, New York. In 1998, I was baptized and became a Christian.

At the same time, my opportunities in educational leadership grew: I became a principal of Link Community School in Newark, and then moved to Denver, Colorado in 2004 to become the founding leader of DSST Public Schools, a charter school network.

Through Tim's teaching, I learned how to be a non-profit leader who honors my faith and my vocation. I learned how to sustain myself in vocation. In this piece, I want to share Tim's contribution to my vocational journey as in three lessons: how to think, how to lead, and how to sustain.

HOW TO THINK

All human beings are driven by "an inner compulsion to understand the world as a meaningful cosmos and to take a position toward it."[1]

Tim taught me how to think. Much of my formal education pales in comparison to the "classroom" that was Tim's pulpit on Sunday morning. His approach, which was grounded in apologetics, was counter to what has been a growing movement in the American church that increasingly treats experiential, life-changing moments as the assumed path to God. In an article for the *New Yorker,* Michael Luo noted that the traditional intellectual strand of Christianity led by the likes of Reinhold Niebuhr in America and C.S. Lewis in England was replaced with more charismatic and experiential expectations of how to find God. He wrote, "In place of belief that a life devoted to God must begin with a sudden, life-changing religious experience, evangelicals should understand that it can unfold in a more gradual process."[2]

This approach has marginalized an intellectual tradition of Christian faith that I needed. As a seeking Christian, I believed the narrative that God was going to come crashing into my life. I was waiting for some big experience where faith would happen. It did not come. Rather, God gave me Redeemer and Tim's teaching, which was centered in a more intellectual approach to the gospel. My faith unfolded in a gradual process of exposure and experiences of God's truth through prolonged thought exercises where God's love, truth, and power were revealed to me. How did this happen?

Tim has a unique ability to present a set of beliefs and support those beliefs with biblical texts and the canon of philosophy, while pulling in a *Village Voice* story from the week before to cement its application in our lived experience. It was a master class on thinking. He has a compassionate and deeply insightful way of thinking through the gospel and how it plays out in modern culture. He draws out implicit and faulty assumptions around the existence of God and points out the inconsistent ways we or others live according to our faith propositions. He models how to explicate the thorniest theological or ethical arguments with humility. No objection is left dangling, and no conclusion is laid heavy on our chests without room to consider its merits in the quiet of our brains and prayer.

And yet, in all of this, Tim leaves plenty of space for the beautiful mystery of faith to fill our hearts and minds. He does not claim truth that only God can. He leaves enough space for us to realize we will never explain or understand the full majesty of God, even as he helps us approach this mystery with a thoughtful confidence.

Learning how to think has had many implications for me in the vocational space. Here are three.

First, Tim Keller taught me that the gospel is not just "faith" practiced on Sunday or when we "need" God in our lives, but that understanding the gospel is integral to a coherent worldview. Our faith lays claim to all aspects of our lives, our vocation included. Prior to coming to Redeemer, my life was compartmentalized, with family and vocation at the center. Faith was a private matter of the heart. This felt particularly true in New York City, where faith was seen as a part of your upbringing, a cultural tradition, but certainly not a "modern" source of truth capable of calling the shots in your life. Compartmentalizing faith seemed to be like a skill every New Yorker needed to master.

I also viewed faith as something needed when things weren't going quite right. One of Tim's most powerful thought exercises came from his sermon "The Gospel and Your Self."

In 1970 a Sunday school teacher changed my life with a simple illustration.

My teacher said, "Let's assume the distance between the earth and the sun (92 million miles) was reduced to the thickness of this sheet of paper. If that is the case, then the distance between the earth and the nearest star would be a stack of papers 70 feet high. And the diameter of the galaxy would be a stack of papers 310 miles high."

Then she added, "The galaxy is just a speck of dust in the universe, yet Jesus holds the universe together by the word of his power."

Finally, the teacher asked her students, "Now, is this the kind of person you ask into your life to be your assistant?"[3]

Jesus is either the Lord of all your life, or none of it.

By integrating the gospel into the moral, political, and cultural issues of our time, Tim has brought a Christian worldview to life embedded in the here and now. He is as likely to quote the *New York Times* as he is theological criticism. And by threading the gospel through the cultural construct of New York, he has modeled for me how to consciously think and how to challenge myself to integrate the Gospel into ALL of my life. The immediate implication of this teaching is that my vocation—what I do, how I do it, and with whom—matters. My approach to work must become aligned to my approach to Christian life.

Second, Tim's teaching of the gospel helped me develop the capacity to engage, think, and make coherent meaning of the tensions of leadership within the context of my own sin. Leadership is a perilous journey, complicated by the polarization of our world, the fragmentation of institutions, and the general lack of trust in authority. When tackling issues such as equitable public education or racial justice, competing values and interests inevitably surface. By giving me the tools to view these conflicts through the lens of my own sin, Tim equipped me to seek what is right without holding too tightly to my own views while leading in the arena.

Third, Tim showed me that the gospel can be explicated in such a way to critique the culture and speak into workplaces and leadership styles. When I came to New York, I believed that the intellectual underpinnings of Christianity were shaky, soft, and did not hold up to "rigorous thought." I believed that Christianity's claims were based on outdated convention, morals, and faith in something that could not be defended. And certainly the gospel had little to say about how to successfully work and lead in high-powered organizations. This serves as an easy partition between faith and vocation. Vocation is concrete—what you do to make a living, where you accomplish your goals and build a career. Faith is a private heart matter that you do not bring to work. But Tim models that the gospel has an important critique on culture, particularly in workplaces, not the other way around. As Lesslie Newbigin writes, "Before you explain the Gospel to the culture, you need to explain and critique the culture with the Gospel"[4]

Tim has presented a framework of thought, an intellectual rigor with the gospel that has helped me coherently critique the culture and reorient my worldview to a more holistic, aligned, and intellectually dependable position. This has been critical for me to bridge the gap from Sundays to the workplace. I started to see how humility, forgiveness, love, and truth could not only be applied to our work, but *must* be applied. My faith lays claim to how I work, pushing me into uncomfortable spaces and questions. Ultimately, Tim has given me a framework that equips me to lead in a way that is consistent with my faith and values, and with other people's longings. This framework is often at odds with the prevailing American work culture of results and self-promotion at all costs.

Through the truths of the gospel, and the model of Tim's teaching, I have been given the tools and a way to think. I have been able to develop an imperfect but cohesive view of *how* to live an aligned life in the private and public squares. I came to New York in search of God and a career and left with a kingdom vocation.

HOW TO LEAD

But if the purpose of work is to serve and exalt something beyond ourselves, then we actually have a better reason to deploy our talent, ambition, and entrepreneurial vigor—and we are more likely to be successful in the long run, even by the world's definition.[5]

Gaining a gospel frame of vocation is just the beginning. How to apply this understanding in day to day leadership is where things can get difficult. How do you apply gospel love when performance can be the difference between organizational failure and thriving? How do you love someone who is underperforming and hurting the rest of the team? Through the discipleship of Redeemer, three important truths have emerged for me on how we lead as Christians.

How you work is important as what you accomplish

> To be a Christian in business, then, means much more than just being honest or not sleeping with your coworkers. It even means more than personal evangelism or holding a Bible study at the office. Rather, it means thinking out the implications of the gospel worldview and God's purposes for your whole work life—and for the whole of the organization under your influence.[6]

Christian leaders are called to care about *how* we do our work as much as the results of our work. The ends rarely, if ever, justify the means. In the non-profit world, one might expect this to be commonplace and not counter-cultural. That has not been my experience. As in the for-profit sector there is a bottom-line mentality in the non-profit world. The need to raise funds, garner additional resources, recruit staff, and build brands has fed a bottom-line mentality that feels necessary to survive. Additionally, a blind adherence to the mission and its intended good is often used to justify organizational cultures that treat people poorly or with disdain in the name of this greater good. As a result, *how* the mission is accomplished is often set to the sideline.

The gospel convicted me early in my leadership journey that we must strive to do our work in ways that honor the way we work. Leaders should ensure that an organization lives its values first as a prerequisite to pursuing its mission. Three practices underlie this:

First, putting as much focus on defining how the team works as it does performance goals. Organizations are often laser clear about the profit and impact goals they seek, but they leave fuzzy expectations about how to behave while achieving those goals. Articulating the core values of the organization, the expected behaviors associated with those values, and the clarity that living these values is as important as the organization's performance outcomes. Second, you get what you honor. Honoring those who live the values of organization, through promotions and recognition, sends clear messages that *how* the work is done is deeply valued. Lastly, when shortcuts present themselves or when things are not going well, re-centering on the values must come before addressing performance. Values are not pithy statements and reminders that make us feel good in times of flourishing. Rather, they are the bedrock of the organization and the results are an expression of them being lived well.

In the end, the gospel calls us to be stewards of the kingdom on earth. And to be good stewards, Christian leaders must care deeply about how they accomplish the work even when that work is for a social good.

Hold Truth and Love Together

Love without truth is sentimentality; it supports and affirms us but keeps us in denial about our flaws. Truth without love is harshness; it gives us information but in such a way that we cannot really hear it.[7]

As a young Christian non-profit leader, one of my early crises of confidence was learning how to love the people I lead, while still holding them accountable to achieving the organization's mission. I had embraced the good news of the gospel, the grace that comes with it, and Jesus' greatest commandment to love your neighbor as yourself. I also knew how sinful I was and was grappling with Jesus' teaching on pride: "You hypocrite, first take the log out of your own eye and then you will see clearly to take the speck out of your brother's eye" (Matt. 7:5). How do I balance my own sin with the requirements of leadership, and the command to love people with the need to get results?

As a new school leader, I was responsible for managing a team of teachers and staff members who would serve our students and families with excellence. Providing our students with a great education was, in many cases, a key to their future and an important way out of the systemic racism and classism of our country. Our teachers and leaders needed to be excellent. So how could I love our staff, truly honor them as human beings (particularly those who were underperforming), while maintaining the integrity of our commitment to our students and families?

I sought Tim's wisdom on this question in 1996, a conversation I have not forgotten twenty-five years later. Over a sandwich in the Redeemer office in mid-town, Tim and I explored these questions of faith and leadership. We both agreed that the gospel holds that one can honor truth and love at the same time. But how do you this in the pragmatic day-to-day of leadership? Here is what we came up with:

It starts with the heart and posture of the leader. A Christian leader needs to lead from a place of humility—a recognition that we all have blind spots and weaknesses. Being open, vulnerable, and embracing one's weaknesses publicly is an important first step. A leader must cultivate a culture of growth and model asking for feedback. All of this establishes a foundation to lead with integrity.

A Christian leader is called to hold truth and love together in decision making. The workplace is not a transactional place, rather a place where we strive to fully honor both people and the mission. We hold what is best for the employee and what is best for the organization coherently together in decisions. We hold team members accountable for their performance, yet we do so in love. This is the place where the gospel calls us to a higher standard. A leader must commit himself fully to helping an underperforming employee meet the performance standard. Typically, underperforming employees are told they are underperforming and sent off to "prove" themselves and "fix it" alone. Christian leaders are called to fully come alongside and share the success or failure of that improvement. We are to fully invest in the process of improvement, not just the outcome.

If the employee does not meet the standard, we can terminate with love, knowing we did everything we could within reason to support them. This process honors the individual and the mission of the organization, the team, and those you serve. Applying the gospel to leadership in this way is not easily done. Nuances are hard to manage and I have, with the best of intentions, made many mistakes along the way. The prevailing culture offers easy ways out as it pushes us to take short cuts at the expense of the employee.

Center on Vulnerability and Persuasion, not Fear and Power

The gospel calls us to lead differently. As a Christian, I understand the extent of my own sin, my own weakness, and that I am saved by the grace of God, not by anything I have done. There is nothing I can do to earn Jesus' love. It requires humility and vulnerability to recognize that I need His saving grace. Jesus modeled this vulnerability in the garden of Gethsemane and on the cross. And countless times throughout the Gospels, Jesus modeled vulnerability, granting people free will and agency when He could have forced them to do what He wanted. He rarely used power to compel, fear to control, His "title" to condemn. Rather He led with love and persuasion. And like Jesus, we are called as Christians to lead with humility and vulnerability in the workplace.

As leaders, we are called to use our titles—and the power such authority brings—sparingly. In his seminal work, *Good to Great,* Jim Collins writes about Level 5 leadership, which "demonstrates a compelling modesty, shunning public adulation; never boastful.... [It] channels ambition into the company, not the self."[8]

Living out Christian faith in the workplace call us to this kind of Level 5 leadership. We often discount God's leadership wisdom. It takes a secular view like Jim Collin's Level 5 leadership concept, which mimics a gospel view of leadership, to validate God's wisdom in our own minds. Tim taught me how to make these connections and see gospel wisdom in secular thinking. Leading with persuasion, humility, and unassuming effectiveness is the call of the gospel. But we often take the short cut of using fear, power, and title. Tim's teaching taught me the difference between the two and provided me the tools to begin to grow into this kind of leadership.

HOW TO SUSTAIN

> The gospel frees us from the relentless pressure of having to prove ourselves and secure our identity through work, for we are already proven and secure.[9]

Sustaining ourselves in vocation is hard in a world often defined by burn out. Success is fleeting, and pressure mounts when one needs to continually prove oneself in the "what have you done lately" culture. The gospel gives us a framework for sustainable leadership. While at Redeemer, I learned to constantly return to the question of whom I am serving in my work. Guarding the intentions of the heart is a daily act of reflection and prayer, because even the best of our intentions can be gradually twisted when it feels like we must prove ourselves every day. Tim Keller writes,

> The human heart is an "idol factory" . . . [that] takes good things like a successful career, love, material possessions, even family, and turns them into ultimate things. Our hearts deify them as the center of our lives, because, we think, they can give us significance and security, safety and fulfillment, if we attain them.[10]

The very good we are doing, our very pride in being an effective Christian leader can be our biggest problem. The human heart has the greatest capacity to twist God's gifts and blessings into idols. The highly successful leader can make achievement an idol, just as the good "Christian leader" can idolize doing the "how" right. In both cases, we allow the idol to become the object of our hearts, rather than honoring God with the gifts He has given us.

I have found this to be particularly true for the founding leader of an organization. There is no more dangerous road to walk than to start a church, a non-profit, or a company. The creation itself becomes the idol, drawing all of our focus and energy to it, not the Creator. Quickly it can go from creating a social good to creating the idol of your life. And this idol can encompass not just the praise and satisfaction that comes with success, but also the pride of succeeding in a godly way. (i.e you doing it better than anyone else. Soon you constantly face the question, am I doing this for the kingdom, for His glory or mine? Has my pride become my center? After pouring ten to fifteen years into an idea, a team, or a mission, the human heart justifies all this sacrifice by claiming ownership.

Tim's teaching was at its best when he addressed idols. He transformed the way I understood idols, from statues of worship in an ancient culture to concrete realities of my heart. He helped me understand that even the best "missional" parts of our lives can become our largest obstacles to faithfully living and leading in the gospel. He taught me that we should not hold on too hard to the results we seek in life, because they will never satisfy but will lead us to longing only for more.

I will never forget Tim using the illustration of actor Tim Allen from the TV show *Home Improvement*. At one point in the early 1990s, Tim Allen had the #1 bestselling book, #1 rated TV show, and #1 top grossing movie all at the same time. In a sermon, Tim Keller quoted an interview with Tim Allen, where he said that, despite being on top of the world, reaching the pinnacle of success and fame as an artist, he had never been less happy and satisfied in his life. This illustration has helped me when I have struggled to keep perspective. Our idols (success in this case) can never satisfy our deepest longings. The truth that they often work in reverse and instead bring us misery has always stuck with me. It has helped me engage in my ongoing work to keep Jesus at my center, not my idols.

CONCLUSION

I have a pretty clear idea of how my ideas have generated enormous revenues for the companies that have used my research; I know I've had a substantial impact. But as I've confronted this disease, it's been interesting to see how unimportant this impact is to me now. I've concluded that the metric by which God will assess my life isn't dollars but the individual lives that I have touched.[11]

Clayton Christensen, a Harvard Business School professor and highly respected management thinker, wrote the piece "How to Measure Your Life" soon after he was diagnosed with cancer. He wrote it for his students who longed for meaning in their lives as they pursued careers after Harvard. Christenson was a believer, and wrestled with how to best apply the gospel to his vocation his whole life.

I have been on a similar journey. The idols of success, collective impact, and professional respect have had an ongoing grip on my heart over my thirty-year career. But I have not been alone on this journey. Like so many other people, I've been repeatedly convicted and encouraged by Tim's teaching. I have been given the tools to understand and apply the gospel, and the maturity to accept what can't be understood. Tim has equipped me to embrace prayer and reflection, and he has given me the desire to keep asking the right questions to integrate my life into a single journey of faith.

ENDNOTES

1   Timothy Keller, *Walking with God through Pain and Suffering* (New York: Riverhead Books, 2013), 14.
2   Michael Luo, "The Wasting of the Evangelical Mind," *New Yorker,* March 4, 2021, https://www.newyorker.com/news/daily-comment/the-wasting-of-the-evangelical-mind.
3   Timothy Keller, "The Gospel and Your Self" (sermon), Redeemer Presbyterian Church, November 13, 2005, https://gospelinlife.com/downloads/the-gospel-and-your-self-5433/.
4   Lesslie Newbigin, *Missionary Theologian: A Reader* (Grand Rapids, MI: Eerdmans, 2006)
5   Timothy Keller and Katherine Leary Alsdorf, *Every Good Endeavor: Connecting Your Work to God's Work* (New York: Penguin, 2012), 57.
6   Keller and Alsdorf, *Every Good Endeavor,* 168.
7   Timothy and Kathy Keller, *The Meaning of Marriage: Facing the Complexities of Commitment with the Wisdom of God* (New York: Penguin, 2010), 44.
8   Jim Collins, *Good to Great: Why Some Companies Make the Leap . . . and Others Don't* (New York: HarperCollins, 2001), 36.
9   Keller and Alsdorf, *Every Good Endeavor,* 63.
10 Timothy Keller, *Counterfeit Gods: The Empty Promises of Money, Sex, and Power, and the Only Hope that Matters* (New York: Penguin Books, 2009), xvi.
11 Clayton M. Christensen, "How Will You Measure Your Life?", *Harvard Business Review,* July—August, 2010, https://hbr.org/2010/07/how-will-you-measure-your-life.

JENNY C. **CHANG**

Mercy

BEING GOD'S SHEPHERDS TO THOSE IN NEED

Ubi caritas et amor, Deus ibi est.

I learned of this wonderful fourth-century church hymn from John, a lawyer who fell on hard times and ended up needing help from the Redeemer Diaconate. Translated, it means: "Where charity and love are, God is there." He was sharing his testimony of what Redeemer Presbyterian Church of New York City meant to him.

When the Kellers first started Redeemer, they brought with them a strong vision for mercy ministries because they were eager to live out the gospel in both word and deed. While many Presbyterian churches around the world give their diaconate the important function of stewarding the church's assets (e.g., property and funds), Tim and Kathy followed the model of diaconates in the Dutch Reformed churches and decided from the beginning to task the church deeks (our affectionate term for deacons and deaconesses) with taking care of the practical needs of the people, focusing especially on serving the needy and providing pastoral care. After all, this was the topic of Tim's doctoral dissertation, which ended up being *Ministries of Mercy,* the very first book he published.

Consider how Tim defines mercy ministry:

> The ministry of mercy is the meeting of "felt" needs through deeds. As agent of the kingdom, the church seeks to bring substantial healing of the effects of sin in all areas of life, including psychological, social, economic, and physical.[1]

While drawing strengths from the skills of modern social work—and Christians were very much at the forefront of modern social work development—Tim makes it clear that church-based ministry is to provide holistic care by seeking to accomplish, through deeds, greater restoration from the brokenness of our sins and of this world. And while I know that after Adam and Eve, every one of us is a sinner and broken, I initially neglected to see how a materially affluent congregation such as Redeemer— filled with doctors, lawyers, and bankers—would have people with needs.

As a regular attender at Redeemer, I was drawn in by Tim's profound teaching. He preached the gospel with a strong sense of urgency that reflected his own robust and intimate walk with the Lord. And when a deaconess friend encouraged me to apply for a position with the diaconate, I was floored to learn that there was already a social worker leading the diaconate full time and working on the initial setup of the ministry. I had never encountered any other church with a church-based social service center as its diaconate. But the question remained: Why would an affluent church need a diaconate—a mercy ministry?

Tim describes the character of mercy and human needs in this way:

> Grace has to do with man's merits, but mercy has to do with man's misery. Theologians have discerned that God's mercy (the Greek word *eleos*) is that aspect of his nature which moves him to relieve suffering and misery. "Mercy" is the impulse that makes us sensitive to hurts and lacks in others and makes us desire to alleviate them. These "hurts or lacks" we call needs.[2]

To some extent we have been culturally conditioned to think that having material wealth equates to having fewer problems, but even those in the upper echelon have hurts or lacks, and they too need encouragement, accountability, and the hope of the gospel. Because Redeemer was a large, multisite church, what I superficially observed and experienced was only a segment of the church. Many congregants, myself included, were guilty of preferring to remain within our comfort zone. This highlighted a lack of humility, as we failed to recognize the contributions that others who were different from us could and would make to the body of Christ.

A COUNTERCULTURE

New York City is known as the financial capital of the world. It is home to Wall Street, two of the largest stock exchanges in the world, many major banks, and other financial institutions. Tim illustrates how financial metrics such as cost/benefit analysis and return on investment have seeped into our daily lives:

> We do a little arithmetic all the time. In every transaction we say, "Is this going to help me? Is this going to profit me? Are these the kind of people I want to be around? Is this the sort of thing that will enhance my portfolio? Is this the sort of thing that will enhance my emotional capital?" Everything is centripetal. We're always thinking inward. We're looking inward. In fact, Martin Luther defines *sin as homo incurvatus in se,* which means humanity curved in, focused inward on itself.[3]

This self-centeredness drives us to make sure our needs are met first, and it makes us less interested in being asked to serve. Furthermore, not only do we make these calculations regarding how we invest our time, energy, and resources; we also calculate who is worthy of help and investment, a notion reflected by the rich young ruler's question "Who is my neighbor?" (Luke 10:29).

In many of Tim's sermons, he preached about what it means to be a chosen people, a royal priesthood, a holy nation, and a people belonging to God. He urged us to not view the church as a social club or a lecture hall but rather as a counterculture. Very early on he talked about the church being "a pilot plant of what humanity would be in every area under the lordship of Christ. Christians are a counterculture. Not a subculture, a counterculture."[4]

The Redeemer Diaconate was a community built on causes that were higher than its individual members, and it served as an example of a counterculture. We were united by mercy, we spurred one another on to focus on commitments that were more important than personal fulfillment and happiness, and we regularly confessed and repented toward being more readily inclined to help those who appeared to have an achievable path to self-sufficiency.

This countercultural notion permeated Redeemer with the hope of influencing the city. As the church grew, an increasingly formalized structure was needed to organize the work of the diaconate. Given the immense size of the city, the diaconate evolved to focus primarily on serving those within the Redeemer church family while other church and parachurch ministries positioned themselves to reach out to and serve the city at large. The Center for Faith & Work (started by Katherine Alsdorf), Redeemer Counseling Services (led by Judy Cha), and Hope for New York (founded by Yvonne Sawyer) are a few key examples of Redeemer's outward-facing ministries. That being said, the scope of the diaconate greatly expanded after disasters like 9/11, the Great Recession of 2008, Hurricane Sandy in 2012, and most recently the COVID-19 pandemic. During these particularly trying times in our city, the diaconate was able to respond to the needs of not only those within our church family but also to many other individuals and families in the city who suddenly found themselves in crisis.

But it was more than just those serving in ministries who strived to be countercultural. We consistently saw a dramatic increase in Mercy Fund offerings after each disaster. Every time we would think "These are economically the worst times we've ever seen in New York City," an abundance of financial gifts would pour in. What was going on? It was the evidence of Christians experiencing grace individually, living counterculturally, and creating a radical community of love and sharing.

OUR FATHER'S FLOCK

On the surface, the diaconate client work resembles social work case management in that it is a collaborative process through which a case manager assesses, plans, and provides the services required to meet the client's needs. (We called them "clients" to convey that while they are our sisters and brothers in Christ, we are also in a committed partnership working for their well-being.) But instead of becoming good case managers, we as deeks sought to become good shepherds. Tim often talks about how every single Christian is a shepherd, and every one of us should be out there amongst the lost sheep and the found sheep of the world.[5] This biblical command guides us in how we relate to those we serve, especially in a large urban setting where cynicism feels endemic.

In New York the risk of being infected with cynicism is high because, though New York is a magical place, it is also a tough city with problems of great magnitude and people facing complex issues. It does not take much to inadvertently adopt the cynical attitude Jonah held toward the inhabitants of Nineveh. There were times that we as a diaconate were skeptical, either of our ability to help or of the stories we were told. How do we guard ourselves against becoming cynical and through our actions help those we serve to thrive? Jesus places great significance on being a good shepherd. What was an acceptable loss of a typical shepherd's flock back in His days? Perhaps up to twenty percent? But a good shepherd lays down his life for his flock and goes after the one that is lost. Often our human heart rationalizes, saying, "Up to twenty percent, that is expendable," but the Spirit in us says, "This is my Father's flock we are looking after; it is precious. Don't lose a single one." Looking back, I am humbled and amazed by how deeks persistently pursued every sheep.

The goal of being good shepherds shaped our helping relationship with our clients. We would ask our clients to provide a full disclosure of their circumstances, which may have felt intrusive. But God is concerned with our whole being, so in order to extend help that would produce lasting results, we asked our clients to let us into their whole lives. Expounding on Acts 20:28, "Pay careful attention to yourselves and to all the flock, in which the Holy Spirit has made you overseers, to care for the church of God, which he obtained with his own blood," Tim stresses the spiritual responsibility we have to respect the highly personal and sensitive information our clients share with us. This served as the overarching principle in the creation of the diaconate's confidentiality agreement, which each deek would abide by.

LET MERCY LIMIT MERCY

Ideally we preferred to wait to close cases after clients' concerns were resolved and needs were met; however, Tim suggests that there are times when we need to limit help if it is unmerciful to continue it. "It is unmerciful to bail out a person who needs to feel the full consequences of his own irresponsible behavior."[6] Tim reframes this concept of "let mercy limit mercy" pastorally:

When God's grace first comes to us, it comes unconditionally, regardless of our merits. But though God's mercy comes without conditions, it does not proceed without conditions! God demands our cooperation in sanctification. Why? Because he loves us, and we can only be happy if we are holy.[7]

As a diaconate, we learned to check in with the Spirit by asking, "Will our assistance for this person help them grow spiritually instead of promoting sin or irresponsibility in them?"

Yes, there are times we must let mercy limit mercy, but we must not do so out of revenge, selfishness, or defensiveness. And we do so by modifying our help (e.g., more emotional and prayerful support in lieu of continued financial aid), not by discontinuing or withdrawing it. In rare cases when we did have to limit mercy, sometimes we saw a positive outcome almost immediately; other times we sadly ended up parting ways. But we always tried to leave the door open in case our clients wanted to come back.

MOBILIZING AND GROWING THE MINISTRY

It has been a great source of joy participating in the diaconate and watching its impact grow through the obedience of God's people and the use of resources He has entrusted to us. Each year we asked church members to help identify those in the church family who have a mercy gifting and nominate them to serve on the diaconate. These candidates would then go through a process of evaluations, interviews, great training, more interviews, and a prayerful decision-making period before being voted in and installed as deeks. The beauty of the body of Christ is that we are all uniquely gifted and created in God's image, and we contribute in different ways to the body. Because we all have strengths and weaknesses—and because we may also go through seasons of varied time and emotional availability—our deeks always worked in pairs.

Though all of us are gifted with grace, we need "the shepherds and teachers, to equip the saints for the work of ministry, for building up the body of Christ" (Eph. 4:11–12). Serving on the diaconate does expose us to suffering—clients' suffering, and at times our own—which is why we met regularly as a corporate body for a time of equipping and mutual support. The equipping segment of our monthly meeting was the "continuing education" portion, offering additional training and resources that are useful in client care work. On multiple occasions Tim and Kathy made themselves available to be our equipping shepherds in order to further equip us spiritually. In an effort to steward our servant leaders well, we always encouraged our deeks to prioritize self-care, protect their Sabbath, and regularly check for signs of burnout.

In addition to relying on our human resources, the diaconate also took up an annual special offering, and God's people always responded so generously. It is out of this Mercy Fund that we were able to participate in God's restoration and bring His shalom to this world by providing stability for members of the body of Christ.

THROUGH PRAYERS

In Colossians 4:12 we read, "Epaphras, who is one of you, a servant of Christ Jesus . . . always struggling on your behalf in his prayers, that you may stand mature and fully assured in all the will of God." The growth of this ministry's impact would not have happened without a team of Epaphrases interceding and praying for the diaconate and the clients we were serving. Upon recognition that deeks who were already ministering on the frontline both needed to be prayed for and did not need to be enlisted in yet one more service area, a team of intercessors was assembled for committed, intentional daily prayer for the diaconate (and for each of the other Redeemer ministries). Those of us on the diaconate regularly stayed in touch with our prayer team to keep them up to speed on the vision God had given, and to let them know for whom they could specifically pray. It was comforting and humbling to be prayed for so consistently.

THIS IS HOW WE KNOW

Many churches across the country and around the world have contacted Redeemer over the years to inquire about how we run and minister through our diaconate—evidence of the diaconate's wide influence beyond the Redeemer community. My enormous admiration goes out to the Kellers for their strong conviction and commitment to mercy ministries, and my deep gratitude to them for entrusting me to equip and support the deeks as well as implement and operationalize their vision. Reflecting back on my fifteen years as the Diaconate Director, it truly feels like heaven on earth to have supernaturally experienced firsthand how God knows who I am, loves me, trains me, gives me friends/community and education/credentials, provides connections and mentoring, and then allows me to do things I never dreamed of doing. And I know I speak on behalf of hundreds of deeks and thousands of diaconate clients who wish to communicate to the Kellers their affection and appreciation. John, the client I mentioned at the beginning of this essay, is just one of many countless lives that have been enriched and transformed by the ministries of Redeemer. Grace does change everything.

Back to John: he fell apart, and let everything that mattered in his life—family, friends, faith, his law practice, even his health—slide. He went on to live a life that, as he put it, "would have shamed the Prodigal Son." On the brink of despair, John was led by God to Redeemer and then to the diaconate. We responded by pouring out our lives to him. That is what the diaconal work is all about, and that is how we know we are recipients of Jesus' grace: when we live the way He lived.

John's life actually came together; his ex-wife and children experienced healing. We knew it had to be through the power of God because we saw a transformation that far exceeded the work we put in. Here we were on the diaconate just trying to do our best, and we saw the transformation, and we knew it was God—that He is our source of healing and strength. God comes down and meets us. This is the answer to "Is God real?" We cannot explain why, but yes, God is real to us. This is how we know!

ENDNOTES

1   Timothy Keller, *Ministries of Mercy: The Call of the Jericho Road* (Phillipsburg, NJ: P&R, 1989), 34.
2   Ibid.
3   Timothy Keller, "The Whirlwind of Jesus" (sermon), Redeemer Presbyterian Church, January 9, 2009, https://gospelinlife.com/downloads/the-whirlwind-of-jesus-5121/.
4   Timothy Keller, "Peace of the King" (sermon), Redeemer Presbyterian Church, August 20, 1989, https://gospelinlife.com/downloads/peace-of-the-king-5590/.
5   Keller, *Ministries of Mercy*, 125.
6   Keller, *Ministries of Mercy*, 78.
7   Keller, *Ministries of Mercy*, 76.

CJ **QUARTLBAUM**

Legacy

EVERY GOOD ENDEAVOR

I guess you can say I came across Tim Keller "late" in life. While I've been in church since I was in my mother's womb, I haven't been a Christian for nearly as long—that didn't happen until I was twenty-two—because being in church doesn't make you a Christian any more than being in a garage makes you a car. The first time I had ears to hear the gospel, I heard it from two major players in the Reformed scene. At the time, I didn't know what "Reformed" meant because I grew up on the other end of the theological spectrum. And I certainly didn't have any idea who this Tim Keller guy was that I heard referenced often, but apparently he was one of the biggest pastors in my city.

Naturally, I had to investigate. I took the trip uptown to Redeemer. It was cool but wasn't for me. Being a young Black guy from Brooklyn, I didn't quite fit the aesthetic. Nevertheless, I really began to enjoy Keller's preaching and teaching. I listened to his sermons regularly and read his books. That's when I came across *Every Good Endeavor.* This book rocked my world. Let me give you a little background to help you understand why.

If you had asked me when I was ten what I wanted to do when I was an adult, my answer would have been simple: write and be left alone. Upon declaring my intentions to major in journalism in college, I was met with a hard *no* from my mother. Being an immigrant, single mother of three, she didn't want to see me struggle in the ways that she did. Therefore, she wanted me to do something that would "make money."

With this in mind, I went to college for finance. I figured a career on Wall Street would be fine and lucrative enough. But through a combination of not enjoying finance, not being good at it, and hearing the gospel just a year into my journey, I very quickly figured out that this wasn't the career for me.

Hearing the gospel and having it change my heart is the single biggest thing to ever happen to me. Nothing before or since has transformed me

Legacy

EVERY GOOD ENDEAVOR

I guess you can say I came across Tim Keller "late" in life. While I've been in church since I was in my mother's womb, I haven't been a Christian for nearly as long—that didn't happen until I was twenty-two—because being in church doesn't make you a Christian any more than being in a garage makes you a car. The first time I had ears to hear the gospel, I heard it from two major players in the Reformed scene. At the time, I didn't know what "Reformed" meant because I grew up on the other end of the theological spectrum. And I certainly didn't have any idea who this Tim Keller guy was that I heard referenced often, but apparently he was one of the biggest pastors in my city.

Naturally, I had to investigate. I took the trip uptown to Redeemer. It was cool but wasn't for me. Being a young Black guy from Brooklyn, I didn't quite fit the aesthetic. Nevertheless, I really began to enjoy Keller's preaching and teaching. I listened to his sermons regularly and read his books. That's when I came across *Every Good Endeavor*. This book rocked my world. Let me give you a little background to help you understand why.

If you had asked me when I was ten what I wanted to do when I was an adult, my answer would have been simple: write and be left alone. Upon declaring my intentions to major in journalism in college, I was met with a hard *no* from my mother. Being an immigrant, single mother of three, she didn't want to see me struggle in the ways that she did. Therefore, she wanted me to do something that would "make money."

With this in mind, I went to college for finance. I figured a career on Wall Street would be fine and lucrative enough. But through a combination of not enjoying finance, not being good at it, and hearing the gospel just a year into my journey, I very quickly figured out that this wasn't the career for me.

Hearing the gospel and having it change my heart is the single biggest thing to ever happen to me. Nothing before or since has transformed me so radically. I knew that a career in finance wasn't going to be it for me. I felt unfulfilled and also like I should be doing something that honored God.

The problem was I had no idea what else I could or should do. I was in my early twenties with limited skills and limited life experience. I dabbled with the idea of being a pastor but as a friend once said to me, "every young evangelical man feels like that's what they should do at some point." I could have very easily taken that route but it just didn't feel right at that moment.

I picked up *Every Good Endeavor* hoping to find some answers. I wanted to do work that was pleasing to God but I didn't really know what that meant. I felt as though the only work that was truly God honoring had to be in the realm of vocational ministry. I also had this idea that work was evil and something we suffer through for forty or fifty years until we can retire.

In the very first chapter Tim teaches us that work is ordained by God and is good:

> In the beginning, then, God worked. Work was not a necessary evil that came into the picture later, or something human beings were created to do but that was beneath the great God himself. No, God worked for the sheer joy of it. Work could not have a more exalted inauguration.[1]

Well, after getting hit with that truth bomb, I still had to figure out what kind of work I would do. I grew up, like many of us, with the belief that some jobs were more important than others. Those were the jobs I wanted. But I love this line from Lester DeKoster's book *Work: The Meaning of Your Life:* "Let city sanitation workers go out this week, and by next week streets are smothered in garbage."[2] A gentle reminder that the unglamorous can still be crucial.

Tim leans on DeKoster's work quite a bit to make his argument for the dignity of work. We tend to prize knowledge work over all others, but I think Tim does an excellent job showing us how that's just wrong:

> What has come down to us is a set of pervasive ideas. One is that work is a necessary evil. The only good work, in this view, is work that helps make us money so that we can support our families and pay others to do menial work. Second, we believe that lower-status or lower-paying work is an assault on our dignity. One result of this belief is that many people take jobs they are not suited for at all, choosing to aim for careers that do not fit their gifts but promise higher wages and prestige. West-

ern societies are increasingly divided between the highly remunerated "knowledge classes" and the more poorly remunerated "service sector," and most of us accept and perpetuate the value judgments that attach to these categories. Another result is that many people will choose to be unemployed rather than do work that they feel is beneath them, and most service and manual labor falls into this category.[3]

This is good, but can I be real? While I can't argue against any of the truth in this passage, it just doesn't read well to the Black kid from Brooklyn—the person whose people are traditionally the last hired and first fired. We are overrepresented in the menial jobs that serve the rich.

It's a little too reminiscent of that old "slaves be happy in your position" theology that was rampant on plantations in the not-so-distant past. Believe me, I understand his sentiments and the truth in them, it just doesn't preach well to my audience. This passage almost turns a blind eye and deaf ear to centuries of injustice.

A few years back some friends and I took a trip to Cleveland to catch a Browns game and a Cavs game. We couldn't help but notice at both sporting events, it seemed we were the only Black faces there to enjoy the games. Nearly every other Black person we saw occupied some service position.

Eventually I struck up a conversation with a group of Black teens working at an ice cream shop. I asked why it seemed as though only White people had disposable income in that city. They proceeded to tell me that the only way for Black people to "make it" was to get out of Cleveland. There was no hope for them if they stayed there.

Statistics bear this out: Cleveland is one of the worst cities for inequality. White workers on average make twice what Black workers make. White workers are disproportionately represented in higher wage occupations while Black workers are disproportionately represented in lower wage occupations. The White poverty rate is only 26% compared to 43% for Black people.

But this is merely a microcosm of the nation at large. The average net worth of a Black family is 10% of a White family's worth; in fact, the average Black family would need 228 years to build the wealth of a White family. The average White household income is $84,000 compared to $51,000 for a Black family. Black people are more than twice as likely to live in poverty and have what amounts to a coin flip's chance of getting out of it, while a White person has a 70% chance.[4] This isn't just about money. I don't know if there is a quality-of-life metric in which Black people in this country don't come out on the lower end of the spectrum on average.

All of this adds up to make messages of "just be happy where you are" and "what you're doing is good" leave a bitter taste in one's mouth. Nevertheless, there is truth to be gleaned in Tim's wise words about the dignity of all work. For those who look like me, who feel trapped in their positions, it's affirming to hear this message that God loves you, sees you, and values the work that you do, and that you can honor Him in it.

For all of us, we can see our work as an act of shaping culture. We get the chance in our work, whatever it is, to leave an impact on this world.

An excellent example of this comes from sportswriter Jonathan Tjarks. He writes for *The Ringer,* one of the biggest sports and culture outlets in the country. At the age of thirty-three, he was diagnosed with a rare form of cancer. After a few weeks he was able to write about his experience.

In his piece, he shared about the anguish of Jesus in the garden of Gethsemane and Jesus' gentle reminder in Matthew 6 that worrying will not add a day to our lives. This is huge. Attitudes at *The Ringer* generally range from agnostic to openly hostile towards Christianity. And yet, Jonathan Tjarks was given an opportunity to influence millions through the telling of his story. A chance that may not have come if he'd never gotten sick.[5]

Our jobs, no matter what they are, represent opportunities to be witnesses in this world. But do we ever consider that? Does the garbage man consider how his collection of trash, and the attitude with which he does it, can be a chance to share the hope he has in Jesus? Or does the ad exec consider how her veto power over the types of ads come out of her company can shape the cultural discourse? Can the teacher see how his work influences our next generation of leaders? *Every Good Endeavor* helped me to work through these issues. All the days and nights I spent working jobs I hated, with people I wasn't very fond of, doing things that were ill fitting for my giftings and skillset—this book served as a reminder that there is good work to be done there for the glory of God and the good of those around me.

One of my last jobs in finance was at a very large bank where I was just another cog in the machine—the lowest point in the hierarchical scale (and they made sure I didn't forget that). I spent ten hours a day on Microsoft Excel doing pivot tables and creating reports. Needless to say, it was mind-numbing for me. But there was a guy I sat next to every day. A rich kid who grew up in a very rich bubble where money was god.

Over the course of our brief time together, we would talk about life,

ENDNOTES

1   Timothy Keller, *Every Good Endeavor: Connecting Your Work to God's Work* (New York: Riverhead Books, 2012), 21.
2   Lester DeKoster, *Work: The Meaning of Your Life* (Grand Rapids, MI: Christian's Library Press, 2015, orig. pub. 1982), 3.
3   Keller, *Every Good Endeavor*, 34–35.
4   Source for these stats
5   Jonathan Tjarks, "The Long Night of the Soul: A story of facing fear, confronting mortality, and turning to faith," *The Ringer*, May 2021, https://www.theringer.com/2021/5/20/22444532/long-night-of-the-soul.

Postscript

ON A LIGHTER NOTE . . .

In addition to all these essays collected to honor the work of Tim Keller, how else can we pay tribute to the Kellers? NYC Broadway style, of course!

Along with the Kellers' strong vision for mercy and justice, cultural renewal through the performing arts had been a part of their bigger vision for a gospel movement in New York City. When Tim pivoted out of his senior pastor role in 2017, the Redeemer Diaconate commissioned Paul Cozby to create a hilarious parody adaptation of the song "I Am the Very Model of a Modern Major-General" from Gilbert and Sullivan's *The Pirates of Penzance* to pay tribute to Tim's character and leadership over the past decades. The modified lyrics are reprinted with permission below:

HE IS THE VERY MODEL OF A MODERN EVANGELICAL

He is the very model of a modern Evangelical
'Twas grace that brought him here 'cause his behavior's not angelical
He knows the Laws and Prophets, and can quote from every one of them,
From Genesis to Malachi no wonder we're all praising him
He's very well acquainted too with matters hermeneutical
And uses them in sermons so most find them therapeutical

We've simply never known a man who is more homiletical
He's preached a million sermons and not one of them heretical
He knows the Gospels up and down and every letter sent by Paul
He knows a thousand hymns and if you ask him he will quote them all
The truth is that he married someone and she *is* angelical
And *that's* why he's the model of a modern Evangelical!

CONTRIBUTORS

KATHERINE LEARY ALSDORF works with churches and global organizations to help them equip and mobilize their congregations for gospel-transformed work in the world. In the midst of her 25-year career in high tech business, she became a believer at Redeemer Presbyterian Church. Ten years later she founded and led Redeemer's Center for Faith & Work and subsequently worked with Tim Keller in the writing of *Every Good Endeavor: Connecting Your Work to God's Work*. She is adjunct faculty for Regent College's MA in Leadership, Theology, and Society program and serves on a variety of boards.

A.D. BAUER is a clergyman in the Reformed Episcopal Church and has pastored both PCA and REC churches. Bauer has taught for Chesapeake Theological Seminary, New Geneva Seminary, and Metro Baltimore Seminary. Alan is the author of *The End: A Reader's Guide to Revelation, The Beginning: A Second Look at the First Sin,* and *How to See: Reading God's Word With New Eyes*. Rev. Bauer lives in Baltimore City with his insightful wife and delights in his four independently minded children, six amazing grandchildren, and one great grand-daughter who is pure sunshine.

J. MARK BERTRAND is a novelist, pastor, and advocate for better Bible design (BibleDesignBlog.com). He has a BA in english literature from Union University, an MFA in creative writing from the University of Houston, and an MDiv from Heidelberg Theological Seminary. Mark is the author of *Rethinking Worldview: Learning to Think, Live, and Speak in This World* and three acclaimed crime novels (*Back on Murder, Pattern of Wounds,* and *Nothing to Hide*). He also contributed to Square Halo's *Bigger on the Inside: Christianity and Doctor Who*.

DAVID BISGROVE is the Senior Pastor of Redeemer Presbyterian Church: West Side in New York City. David has an MBA and a master's in public health from Columbia University and previously worked in healthcare finance and administration. He later received his MDiv from Westminster Theological Seminary. David and his wife, Alice, live on the Upper West Side with their two daughters.

MIKE BONTRAGER has spent his career starting and operating purpose-driven for-profit and non-profit organizations. Mike founded Chatham

Financial and eventually helped shape it as a multiple bottom lines company whose quest was to catalyze and model the restoration of trust in the capital markets. After retiring, he founded Square Roots Collective to partner with both for-profit and non-profit community ventures to pursue a community where everyone has the opportunity to thrive.

NED BUSTARD is a graphic designer, illustrator, and author. Some of the books he has worked on include *It Was Good: Making Art to the Glory of God*, *Bible History ABCs: God's Story from A to Z*, *Revealed: A Storybook Bible for Grown-Ups*, *History of Art: Creation to Contemporary*, *Saint Nicholas the Giftgiver*, and *Every Moment Holy*. He is the creative director for World's End Images, the curator for the Square Halo Gallery, and an elder at Wheatland Presbyterian Church.

JUDY CHA has been the director of Redeemer Counseling Services since 2007. She holds a master of arts and religion in counseling and a PhD in marriage and family therapy. Dr. Cha specializes in the areas of relationships, self-image, and multicultural issues, and has led seminars and workshops related to marriage, parenting, and self-image. She also specializes in integrating spirituality and psychotherapy and has collaboratively worked with clergy and clinical supervisors to develop a spiritually-integrated psychotherapy framework.

JENNY C. CHANG grew up in MD/DC area and realized her childhood dream of living in the city by attending school in New York. Worshipping at Redeemer was life-changing. The events of 9/11 cemented her calling to stay in the city and serve. She became a social worker and got involved with the Redeemer Diaconate, which led to fifteen years of leading the Diaconate. Jenny is in awe of God's desire to extend mercy and ability to heal; only God can dream up a journey like this for her.

WILLIAM EDGAR is Professor of Apologetics at Westminster Theological Seminary, PA, where he has taught for some thirty years. He directs the gospel-jazz band Renewal, which features the legendary singer Ruth Naomi Floyd. Edgar is currently *Professeur Associé* at the Faculté Jean Calvin, Aix-en-Provence. He has published some twenty books and numerous articles, including contributions to Square Halo's art and music *It Was Good* books. William and his wife, Barbara have two children and three grandchildren.

DENIS HAACK co-directed Ransom Fellowship—with his wife, Margie—until his retirement in 2020. He is a frequent speaker at L'Abri conferences, as well as a senior writer for Sage Christianity. His reflections appear on Critique-Letters.com, and he is currently working on a book. He also helps curate an art gallery at Church of the Cross (Anglican). The Haacks live in Savage, MN—a quiet community unlike its name—and have three children, nine grandchildren, and one great-grandson, all of whom are above average.

BILL KURTZ is a husband and father, and Founding CEO of DSST Public Schools in Denver, CO, a network of 16 charter schools serving 7,000 students. He is a member of the National Charter School Hall of Fame and was the 2010 New School Venture Fund Entrepreneur of the Year. He attended Redeemer Presbyterian Church from 1993–2004 and currently is a member of the Denver Presbyterian Church.

SEAN MICHAEL LUCAS serves as senior pastor at Independent Presbyterian Church (PCA), Memphis, TN, and as the Chancellor's Professor of Church History at Reformed Theological Seminary. He is the author or editor of several books, including *The Legacy of Jonathan Edwards: American Religion and the Evangelical Tradition* (co-edited with D.G. Hart and Stephen J. Nichols) and *God's Grand Design: The Theological Vision of Jonathan Edwards*.

RUSSELL MOORE is Public Theologian at *Christianity Today* and Director of *Christianity Today's* Public Theology Project. Dr. Moore is the author of several books, including *The Courage to Stand: Facing Your Fear Without Losing Your Soul, Onward: Engaging the Culture without Losing the Gospel,* and *The Storm-Tossed Family: How the Cross Reshapes the Home.*

ANNIE NARDONE is an author, educator, and bibliophile who holds an MA in cultural apologetics from Houston Baptist University and is a Fellow with the C.S. Lewis Institute. She is on the Founder's Council for The Society for Women of Letters. Her writing can be found in the apologetics quarterly *An Unexpected Journal;* at the online magazine, *Cultivating;* and in Square Halo's *Wild Things and Castles in the Sky.*

CHARLIE PEACOCK is a Grammy Award-winning music producer and recording artist. He co-founded Art House America, Wedgwood Circle, and is the Founder/Director Emeritus of the Commercial Music Program at Lipscomb University. As an author, Peacock has written two books, published articles in *Christianity Today, Keyboard,* and *Comment,* and has contributed chapters to numerous collections, including *It Was Good: Making Art To The Glory Of God.* His diverse musical collaborations include: Ladysmith Black Mambazo, The Civil Wars, Switchfoot, Bela Fleck, John Patitucci, and Chris Cornell.

JOHN PATITUCCI has been at the forefront of the jazz world for over thirty years. He is a four-time Grammy Award winner who has performed and/or recorded with artists such as Dizzy Gillespie, Herbie Hancock, Chick Corea, Stan Getz, Wynton Marsalis, Charlie Peacock, John Mayer, Alicia Keys, Bono, Joni Mitchell, Sting, Norah Jones, James Taylor, Paul Simon, and more. He also has sixteen solo recordings, including *Soul of the Bass* (2019). He was a contributor to *It Was Good: Making Music to the Glory of God* and recently completed his first film score (*Chicago America's Hidden War,* 2021).

DANIEL R. SPANJER is a professor of history and department chair at Lancaster Bible College. He also serves as an elder at Wheatland Presbyterian Church and chair of the Board of Governors for Veritas Academy. He earned a master's of arts in theology from Reformed Theological Seminary and his PhD in American cultural history from the University at Albany, SUNY. He is also the co-creator of LBC's Alcuin Society and the Unlikely Pilgrims podcast.

CJ QUARTLBAUM is a writer and speaker from Brooklyn, NY. He is the founder of the non-profit Labor Forward, which aims to improve the way Black history is taught. He also has a bi-weekly newsletter, Live & Labor, that provides simple teachings on living in the way of Jesus. CJ is passionate about a lot of things but mainly about Jesus, his wife, Meredith, and their three babies—Eilish, Elodie, and Amias. You can follow him on the socials: @CJ_Quartlbaum.

SCOTT SAULS serves as senior pastor of Christ Presbyterian Church in Nashville, TN. Prior to this, he was a Lead and Preaching Pastor at Redeemer Presbyterian in New York City, after planting two churches in Kansas City and Saint Louis. Scott has authored several books, including *Jesus Outside the Lines, A Gentle Answer,* and *Beautiful People Don't Just Happen.* Scott blogs regularly at ScottSauls.com and can be found on Twitter and Instagram at @scottsauls.

CHRIS WHITFORD is the CEO and a founding member of Avail NYC, a non-profit founded in 1996 to serve New Yorkers. Chris is a member of the President's Council for the Gilder Lehrman Institute of American History and participated as a 2021 Praxis Non-Profit Leader Fellow. Over the years, Chris has appeared on podcasts and at events geared toward non-profit and ministry leaders throughout NYC and beyond. Chris is a graduate of Brown University. She and her husband are members of Redeemer Presbyterian Church and residents of the Upper West Side.

OF COURSE MANY SQUARE HALO BOOKS **QUOTE** TIM KELLER ... BUT HE ALSO **WROTE** FOR ONE.

What does it mean to be a creative individual who is a follower of the creative God? The three *It Was Good* books seek to answer that question through essays that offer theoretical and practical insights into artmaking from a Christian perspective. In the first of the series, *It Was Good: Making Art to the Glory of God*, Tim Keller discusses why the church needs artists.